Charlie Parker

CHARLIE PARKER

Brian Priestley

Selected discography
by Brian Priestley

Spellmount
TUNBRIDGE WELLS

Hippocrene Books
NEW YORK

First published in UK in 1984 by
SPELLMOUNT LTD
12 Dene Way, Speldhurst
Tunbridge Wells, Kent TN3 0NX

ISBN 0 946771 00 6

British Library Cataloguing in Publication Data
Priestley, Brian
Charlie Parker.—(The Jazz masters)
1. Parker, Charlie 2. Jazz musicians—
United States—Biography 3. Saxophonists—
United States—Biography
788'.66'0924 ML419.P4

First published in USA in 1984 by
HIPPOCRENE BOOKS INC
171 Madison Avenue
New York, NY 10016

ISBN 0 88254 906 5

Series editor: John Latimer Smith
Cover design: Peter Theodosiou

Printed and bound in Great Britain
by Anchor/Brendon Ltd, Tiptree, Essex

Contents

Acknowledgements

I am most grateful to Alan Cohen, Mark Gardner and Tony Williams for their assistance. As well as being indebted to the sources recommended in the Bibliography, I should like to offer thanks to those musicians who talked with me directly and who are quoted herein.

Illustrations

Cover: Charlie Parker (Max Jones)
Drawing by Mal Dean (Melody Maker)
Title page: Parker with Tommy Potter (David Redfern)

A musical home in the Jay McShann Band: Charlie (third from left) looks down at pianist McShann, Walter Brown is next to him (second from left), Little John Jackson is front and centre, while Gus Johnson and Gene Ramey are second from right and far right respectively. (Ross Russell)

A mid-1940s publicity shot. (Max Jones)

A break in the recording studio. (Max Jones)

The Charlie Parker Quintet: Tommy Potter (bass), Miles Davis (trumpet), the shoulder of pianist Duke Jordan and, half-hidden behind Charlie, drummer Max Roach. (David Redfern)

The 'Quintet of the Year': Bud Powell (piano), Charles Mingus (bass), Max Roach, Dizzy Gillespie and Charlie at Massey Hall, Toronto. (Duncan Schiedt)

Birdland opens with a jam-session of Kansas City stars, Lester Young (tenor), Hot Lips Page (trumpet) and Charlie. (Ross Russell)

Charlie jamming with the expatriate all-stars, Sidney Bechet (soprano) and Don Byas (tenor), during the finale of the Paris Jazz Fair. (Chas Delaunay)

The strings come home to roost at Birdland. (Ross Russell)

Introduction

Like many people who will read this book, I first became aware of Charlie Parker after his death. In my case, as a comparative novice, I had no idea of the connotations of either word in the title *Cool Blues*. But the sound of the record on the radio, and the surprising information that its creator had died at the age of 34, made enough of an impact to outweigh my lack of understanding. Naturally, although the memory of that first hearing is still strong, any such encounter depends on the listener's previous listening (and reading), and it was an awfully long time before I was really able to appreciate Parker's importance as one of the most significant jazzmen ever.

These days, the diversity and the sheer amount of jazz has increased to such an extent that it is quite possible to hear about the man before hearing any of his music. Perhaps a liking for a musical descendant of Parker such as saxophonist Dave Sanborn (or the knowledge that the Weather Report tune *Birdland* was dedicated to the long-defunct New York nightclub called after his nickname 'Bird') may have aroused expectations not entirely satisfied, or in some respects even disappointed, by listening to his records. One reason for this can easily be that so much of Parker's sound and style has entered the present-day mainstream as to make the original seem old-hat, at least initially. This problem usually disappears, however, by the time one has spent sufficient study on the recordings to realize that the altoist was light-years ahead of all but a handful of his contemporaries.

The purpose of this book is to make that fact clear, and also to relate his musical development to his private life. This is never a straightforward relationship – not for any artist who produces anything memorable, that is. It's worth pointing out that, already by the time of Mozart and Beethoven (with whom Parker is comparable in status and influence), the process of creating music was being subtly distorted by the difficulties of earning a living thereby. At least in the mind of the artist himself, the ability to concentrate only on the creation, while sailing unconcerned through life, is sometimes replaced by worries about financial survival with a consequent drain on the energy available for music. Of course, the circumstances under which creation takes place are normally masked by the sublime nature of music itself, and the dramatic contrast between the two is even more striking in the case of Parker, since he was an improviser by profession rather than a composer.

The contrast is also marked in so far as many of Parker's difficulties were ones he brought on himself. It is hard to overestimate the long-term effects of drug abuse, including of course its debilitating financial consequences. And yet this was so prevalent at one time in the jazz world that, as well as a number of fatal victims, we can also find numerous examples of individuals (Miles Davis, Stan Getz, Sonny Rollins and John Coltrane among them) sufficiently strong-minded to have decided after a period of addiction to shun any further involvement. What is noticeable, though, is that all the musicians in the latter category took up hard drugs knowingly in their early twenties or even later, whereas Charlie (like so many youngsters today) became a user while still a teenager and without a knowledge of its eventual effects. As to why he should have been such a willing victim, there were perhaps also extenuating circumstances in his family background, so that the same egotistical drive which enabled him to master the basics of his playing style so rapidly was merely the reverse side of a coin inscribed: 'I am the great Charlie Parker, and I can do anything I want and get away with it.'

Because he appeared to do just that for a while, he became a hero to many white intellectuals and, of course, to fellow blacks who would have loved to beat the 'system'. But he himself was too aware intellectually to be other than pessimistic about American society, as Kenny Dorham among others has pointed out: 'His thing was like he'd just get high and blank that other part out. I guess he saw it wasn't going to get together in his lifetime.' On the other hand, like so many Americans before and since, he hoped that the 'star' system would work to his benefit; his work with a string section brought him more widespread popularity yet, when the limitations of the format became clear, he blamed others. 'He had a great resentment of white management and dictatorship,' said Mercer Ellington, although interestingly Parker never spoke in that vein to whites. Even with those he trusted, he preferred to brush the subject aside, which is in strong contrast to the approach of some other musicians of his generation such as Max Roach and Charles Mingus. They, however, only became fairly vocal because of the gradual change of climate from the mid-1950s onwards, whereas Parker died in 1955.

Whether the idea of thinking in terms of solidarity with others would have come easily is open to doubt. He knew that his own personality, rather than the responsibility towards his art which he also felt, was what condemned him to be a loner, saying to a friend, 'I don't let anyone get close to me. Even you. Or my wife.' And he justified the expenditure required by his extravagant needs, with the words: 'If I saved my money, the wives would take it away from me.' The inevitable, cynical, but also painful conclusion was drawn in the comment to his subsequent biographer Robert Reisner, 'Bread is your only friend.'

Chapter Two

The Charlie Parker who made such an impact on the world of music was in every way a child of Kansas City, in the state of Missouri. But the Charlie Parker who came into the world on August 29, 1920 was brought up, for the first seven years of his life, in Kansas City, Kansas. The suburb was not only beyond the state-line but, during the 1920s at least, quite countrified and relaxed compared to its big-city sister. At this period, Charlie enjoyed a relatively stable family background and attended a local Catholic school, where he even sang in the school choir.

His mother, the former Addie Bayley, had her only child when she was not more than about 17, and also found herself bringing up John Parker, two years older than Charlie and born of an earlier liaison of her husband with a white woman. Charles Parker Sr. had settled in the Kansas City area after travelling the country as a singer and pianist with touring shows of the kind that provided Bessie Smith and others with their livelihood. While he remained married to Addie, he was still working as an entertainer but becoming even more successful at drinking away his earnings. Already Addie was the one who was bringing in the regular money, and it seems unlikely that her husband could even afford his own piano, or any other instrument. Had he done so, we would certainly have heard of young Charles's musical talent at an earlier age.

It was when Parker Sr. moved his family to the centre of town, ostensibly to be nearer to potential employers but probably in order to spend more time carousing, that the household began to break up. By 1930, the father had gone off to live with another woman and, as the Depression hit the entertainment business, he began to travel the country again, this time as a chef on the railways. The financial implications of his continual travelling meant that Addie was now the sole breadwinner and, since her meagre savings had been wiped out in the bank crash, she took a job as a night cleaner to continue paying for their new home. This meant that Charlie was often left in the charge of his half-brother, but the emotional implications were perhaps even more serious. Mrs. Parker's love was centred exclusively on her son, who now channelled his desire for parental affection in the only direction available to him. A parallel can be drawn with the relationship between Billie Holiday and her mother, with the exception that Billie at least met her father again later in life and witnessed his pride in her achievements. Charlie Parker's father was stabbed to death by a woman friend in 1939.

The family move had brought Charlie into the Kansas City public school system but, although at Crispus Attucks School he was a diligent pupil, learning what he was asked to learn without stretching himself, there was still no music-making. He was interested in music, of course, like many of the kids in the ghetto area, and told saxophonist Budd Johnson many years later, 'We were the little cats that played stickball out in front of the house. And when you cats would start to rehearse, we would come up to the window and look in and listen to you guys.' But, if Parker Sr.'s collection of early jazz and blues records was still around the house, there has been no mention of Charlie playing them. It was not until he entered Lincoln High at the age of 11 that the flame was lit which kept him burning for the rest of his life.

Instruction in the cumbersome baritone-horn which he was assigned might have stood him in good stead if he had gone on to specialise in the trumpet or trombone. But participating in the school's marching band and 'symphonic band' did at least fill his head with the pleasing logic of European harmonies, and gave him a taste for the melodies composed for other instruments than the baritone-horn. Playing written music, however, was nothing compared to the benefits of associating with other youngsters in the band such as trombonist Robert Simpson. Simpson, who was some three years older than Charlie, became according to Charlie's mother 'his inseparable friend.' He not only played the written music accurately and with feeling but, out of school hours, he was playing excellent jazz by ear. Pretty soon, Charlie was too and began pestering his mother to buy him an instrument of his own. By the time he was 13, she had saved enough to get a rather decrepit, second-hand alto saxophone and, by the time he was 14, he was taking his first paid engagements with Simpson in a small band called The Deans Of Swing led by another school friend, Lawrence '88' Keyes, who was some five years his senior.

The influence of such grown-up boys was both good and bad. He was able to question Keyes about harmony and see the answers demonstrated on the piano, and to discover that playing jazz was not just a matter of a good ear and a lot of enthusiasm. Even a young amateur band had to meet exacting standards, and Charlie's attendance at school became irregular as he devoted himself to gigging and rehearsing and merely socialising with his companions or occasional girl-friends, who were also older. When he needed to join the musicians' union at 14, he pretended to be 18 and backed it up by dropping out of school altogether. The so-called supervision of his half-brother during the nighttime did little to deter him from hanging around outside places such as the Reno Club, where local hero Count Basie had taken up residence shortly after his employer, bandleader Bennie Moten, had died on the operating table in April 1935: the former Moten bandsmen chosen by Basie included saxophonist Lester Young, soon to gain international fame for his revolutionary but seemingly effortless solos, and who used to smuggle Charlie into the club during the band's breaks. Although far from the remote personality he later became, Lester was 11 years older than Charlie and verbally uncommunicative about his music. To Charlie, he was like a god – a god who sometimes reached down and passed him the marihuana cigarette which circulated (perfectly legally until

1937) on the cramped bandstand.

Even if Charlie was growing up too fast for his own good, the great advantage of doing so in Kansas City at this period was the vast number of outlets for music. Whereas elsewhere in the country the repeal of Prohibition had initially accelerated the slump in night-club business, the gangster-run clubs of K.C. thrived under the town's corrupt administration to such an extent that demand for musicians almost outstripped supply, and club managements were prepared to give anyone a try. 'I tried playing a job at the Orchid Room with my friend Robert Simpson, and they threw us out', recalled Parker. But the forum for being heard by fellow musicians was the jam session, an important institution in the 1930s and nowhere more so than in Kansas City. Charlie became first a keen observer and then an overambitious participant, while he was still a barely competent Dean Of Swing. For his first attempt to sit in on a jam session, at the Hi-Hat Club:

> I'd learned the first eight bars of *Lazy River* and I knew the complete tune of *Honeysuckle Rose*. I didn't ever stop to think about any different kind of keys or nothing like that . . . The first thing they started playing was *Body and Soul*, so I go to playing my *Honeysuckle Rose* and they laughed me off the band stand, laughed at me so hard I had to leave the club.

In later years, the integration of a melodic quotation during an improvisation on another tune (even examples as complex as Louis Armstrong's *West End Blues* introduction or the theme of Charlie Shavers's *Dawn on the Desert*) was to become just one aspect of Parker's fertile imagination and musical self-confidence, but for the moment he had bitten off more than he could chew. Before playing in public again, he practised every day for three months and, at the end of this period, he landed a job with bandleader Tommy Douglas. His improved control of the instrument was put to good use and his knowledge of harmony and repertoire was considerably widened by playing regularly for dancers. Furthermore, Douglas (who later recorded with singer Julia Lee and others) had been conservatory-trained, which was highly unusual for a black musician in those days, and could discuss music with Charlie and provide him with new challenges. No doubt due to Douglas's influence, Charlie came to admire the technical expertise of sax players such as Jimmy Dorsey and even

14

the French 'straight music' virtuoso Marcel Mule. When Douglas lent him a clarinet, a more complex instrument than the saxophone, he was amazed that Charlie mastered the basic differences virtually overnight.

It was now 1936 and, since acquiring his saxophone at 13, Charlie had made up for lost time musically. Intellectually and emotionally, he was still running before he had learned to walk. A considerable appetite for reading, which he felt to be a more adult occupation than school studies had ever been, did not prepare him for a rude shock to his Oedipus complex when he found his mother in bed with a man. It seems revealing that Charlie's outraged and finally understanding reaction was more like that of a deceived husband than a son. And it is surely significant that in the same year he himself became the husband of Rebecca Ruffing, who had been four years ahead of him in school and always had a soft spot for him. In this was a gesture of independence from his mother, it did not prevent him from accepting her offer of housing him and Rebecca – together with *her* mother and several other children! Soon after, the arrival of a son, Leon Francis Parker, augmented the household still further.

What Charlie required from Rebecca was lovemaking and admiration, in other words some confirmation of his self-esteem. That apart, he was content to let mother, substitute mother and mother-in-law get on with it, while he got on with his practising and gigging and sitting-in. Though his ability was increasing rapidly, he was still overreaching himself in jam-session situations and, what is more, gaining a bad reputation for constantly trying ideas he had not really mastered. One night, probably in the summer of 1936, he went so far as to sit in with the major-league men of the Basie band, doubtless with some nodded encouragement from Lester Young. But Basie's brilliant new drummer, Jo Jones, knew of Parker at least by reputation and, waiting till Charlie had just taken off on his solo flight, gunned him down in no uncertain manner: lost in concentration on the music, Charlie was abruptly halted by the resounding crash of the drummer's cymbal thrown at his feet.

Whether or not he took out his frustration and humiliation on Rebecca, things went badly from the start. He expected, but at the same resented, her organising his clothing and his mealtimes as his mother had done and, once when he needed a taxi and Rebecca had no ready money, he pawned his mother's electric iron. (This was merely the first recorded example of a lifetime habit of either borrowing money or pawning his horn, or borrowing a horn from a friend and then pawning the friend's horn – just sometimes, his mother or his friend would be repaid later.) The frequently violent arguments between the young couple can hardly have been helped by having both mothers on the premises, and it must have been with relief that Charlie accepted a three-month engagement in the Ozarks for the summer of 1937 with singer George E. Lee (the then-more-famous brother of Julia Lee). Here, with no distractions apart from the occasional female admirer, Charlie spent whole days studying harmony with the band's pianist and guitarist, and experimenting with it on his single-note instrument. As he ran up and down the chords and scales, and for the first time began to *hear* the relationship between the two, he became utterly dedicated to gaining command of his chosen idiom and in the process laid the basis of his subsequent stunning fluency. The rest of the time, he played and replayed the first records to be issued of Count Basie and Lester Young, learning the solos by heart until he could repeat them himself note for note; he could still do so, privately, in the 1950s.

If this should seem unlikely, given his performance at high school, it should perhaps be remembered that he was born under the sign of Virgo (like Lester, in fact). Traditionally such people are held to be capable, once their interest has been aroused, of infinite attention to detail and of an almost ruthless pursuit of perfection. Sadly, this was also true, in Charlie's case, of his search for the ultimate in stimulants. Kansas City night-club owner Tootie Clarkin commented:

> From nutmeg Bird went to benzedrine inhalers. He'd break them open and soak them in wine. Then he smoked tea [marijuana] and finally got hooked on heroin. He was the only man I knew who could drink with heroin.

He might have gone on to say that Parker's physical make-up was so out of the ordinary that he was one of the rare individuals not to become instantly addicted to something as potent at heroin. For years, he was able to take it or leave it, although on the whole

16

he preferred to take it. Clarkin did add, however, 'When Bird was sixteen he looked 38. He had the oldest-looking face I ever saw'.

Chapter Three

Musically, Charlie Parker had finally got himself together at the age of 17, and the only way to go was up. The fact that the Count Basie band had appeared on records, and were beginning to make it in New York, did not go unnoticed. But, for the moment, no longer being the most unpopular jazzmen in Kansas City became Charlie's incentive for further musical exploration. He found a powerful ally and inspiration in his next bandleader, the altoist and arranger Buster Smith. Known as 'Prof' to his friends, Smith had been a colleague of Basie's off and on since 1928 and had initially been his co-leader at the Reno Club, until going off to do his own thing just before Basie was discovered by New York-based talent scouts. Now, in the autumn of 1937, he had assembled a 12-piece band with Jay McShann on piano and with Parker his second alto player.

It has been suggested that Charlie's personal 'sound' was immediately apparent as soon as he returned from the Ozarks, but it seems more likely that what began to show through was the highly individual architecture of his solos. Buster Smith recalled, 'He'd improved a good bit since I'd seen him before and of course I wanted him. The only trouble he had was with his mouthpiece. He had trouble getting the tone he wanted to get.' What Buster advised Charlie to do was to cultivate power and projection rather than a conventional rounded tone, by using the toughest reeds he could. (He himself described having used a tenor saxophone reed on his alto when Lester Young had a baritone reed on tenor!) The tiny number of records on which Smith played at this period, particularly *Baby Look At You* with Kansas City stalwart Pete Johnson, show some melodic ideas which went into Parker's vocabulary and especially the flexible but slightly edgy tone with which Parker became identified. In fact, Smith's playing is the only thing on record remotely like Parker, before Charlie himself.

Unselfishly, Buster carried Charlie along with him when the band was fronted occasionally by former Moten trumpeter Dee 'Prince' Stewart and, even more surprisingly, kept him on when he obtained a residency at the Antlers club that only required a seven-piece group. 'He always wanted me to take the first solo . . . But after a while anything I could make on my horn he could make too – and make something better out of it.' This comfortable and stimulating partnership only ended when, in September 1938, Smith accepted an offer to do some arranging work in New York for Count Basie, now resident at the Famous Door on 52nd Street. He was aware that employment for musicians in Kansas City had passed its peak and, hoping to make enough contacts in New York to be able to import his own band, promised Charlie that he would send for him in due course. In the meantime, Charlie went to work for Jay McShann's seven-piece group until McShann too found himself, concurrently with the downfall of K.C's political bosses, without a club to play in and went to Chicago for several months. Shortly afterwards, many of the musicians still in Kansas City including Charlie and his heroin connection, a drummer known as Little Phil, were conducting their nightly jam-sessions under the stars in the city's parks.

In addition to the lack of employment, three other reasons have been given for Parker's eventual departure. Around this time, his friend and inspiration Robert Simpson died tragically, also on the operating table. He felt too that it was time to get away from Rebecca, who subsequently divorced him and remarried, leaving Leon in the hands of Charlie's mother. He also felt he was ready to take a look at New York, and apparently his decision was hastened by an argument with a Kansas City taxi-driver in whose cab he ran up a bill of ten dollars, no small sum in those days; during the altercation, he attacked the driver with a knife and was not only arrested but, according to his own account, spent 22 days in prison, and undergoing psychiatric tests. Impatient to shake the hometown dust off his feet, he pawned his saxophone and took a free ride on a freight-train bound for Chicago, where he immediately impressed local musicians by the contrast between his hobo-like appearance and his sophisticated playing. 'And this cat gets up there, and I'm telling you he blew the bell off that thing!' recalled eye-witness Billy Eckstine, adding that the man whose instrument he borrowed, Goon Gardner (later to record with T-Bone Walker), befriended him and lent him some clothes and a clarinet. As a result Parker stayed around and made a few gigs, and connections of another kind. 'According to what Goon told me, one day he looked for Bird, and Bird, the clarinet, and all was gone.'

Shortly afterwards Parker showed up in New York and decided that he was staying with Buster Smith and his wife. Sleeping in their bed during the daytime, he spent the evenings and nights looking for paying gigs and sitting in at jam-sessions. He had, however, not realised the quantity of promising musicians who gravitated to New York City, nor indeed the sheer professionalism in the upper echelons of the jazz business. The soloists who jammed with each other at a top Harlem after-hours spot such as Puss Johnson's (where Coleman Hawkins chose to make his dramatic reappearance later in 1939) overawed Charlie so much that he thought better of trying to play there. And, as far as actual work was concerned, opportunities were severely restricted since the musicians' union in New York was the branch most keen on observing the rule that a new arrival must wait six months before transferring membership from his hometown.

So, when Mrs. Smith put her foot down, he took a non-musical job for the first and only time in his life, washing dishes at Jimmy's Chicken Shack. But the real attraction here was that playing to the audiences out front was the great Art Tatum, the blind solo pianist whose harmonic ingenuity perhaps exceeded Ellington's at this stage and whose speed of execution was so dazzling that the ingenuity was lost on all but the more inquiring of his fellow musicians. The influence of this nightly exposure to Tatum can hardly be overestimated, and it was just at this period that Charlie made a significant discovery while jamming at the Chili House with another devotee of advanced harmony, guitarist Bill (Biddy) Fleet:

Now I'd been getting bored with the stereotyped changes [chords] that were being used all the time . . . I found that by using the higher intervals of a chord as a melody line and backing them with appropriately related changes, I could play the thing I'd been hearing. (See Chapter 8 for further discussion.)

Still officially restricted to non-unionised venues or out-of-town work as far as paid engagements were concerned, Charlie had accepted a gig of several weeks in Maryland with the not very enthralling Banjo Burney when he was summoned home for his father's funeral. As well as feeling under some obligation to stay with his mother and young Leon for a while, Charlie had nothing specific to go back to in New York and had made no close friends apart from trumpeter Bobby Moore who, early the following year, was to be committed to a mental hospital for the rest of his life. Probably also he wanted to spend some time on his home ground following up his Chili House revelation and, after a few unsatisfactory weeks working for Harlan Leonard, he was in the right place at the right time to become a founder member of the new enlarged band assembled in early 1940 by Jay McShann. This band was to provide Charlie with a musical home for the next two-and-a-half years, as well as giving him his first opportunity to make records. (A private recording, so far unissued, of Parker playing *Honeysuckle Rose* and *Body and Soul* entirely unaccompanied is said to have been made in Kansas City in 1937, but in fact sounds too confident and too typical to date from earlier than 1941 or even late in 1943.)

As in his previous working situations, Parker was still the youngest member but the McShann band's average age was younger than the established Kansas City groups. They were inspired by his outstanding ability, not only as a soloist but as an organiser, when he rehearsed the reed section and put together his only known big-band compositions such as *Hootie Blues, Jumpin' Blues* and *Yardbird Suite.* The latter title, never recorded by the McShann band although given a tryout at their first record session, is a reminder that the camaraderie in the band spawned Charlie's nickname 'Yardbird'. Accounts of the actual origin differ, but all except Charlie himself seem agreed that the reference was to a chicken intended for the pot. This later became shortened for general usuage to 'Bird', although Dizzy Gillespie, for one, still refers to him as 'Yard'.

Among the other musicians were the hard-driving bass and

drums teams of Gene Ramey and Gus Johnson; several former Deans Of Swing, including vocalist Walter Brown; and trumpeter Buddy Anderson, whose ideas about altered chords naturally interested Charlie. He himself was one of two altoists and, between him and John Jackson (a forthright blues player as his recorded work on *Dexter Blues* and *Lonely Boy Blues* shows), there was mutual admiration and a piquant contrast – Charlie's own blues solo on *Hootie Blues* was more quizzical and laid-back, like those of Buster Smith. His more overt humour shows through on the *Donkey Serenade* quotation behind the theme of the same number, while his authoritative way of beginning a solo with a striking (often strikingly simple) phrase is reminiscent of Lester Young, for instance on the radio transcriptions of *Lady Be Good* and *Moten Swing*. The combining of these factors in the two-bar pick-up *before* the expected start of his solo space on *Swingmatism* is the sort of thing that bewildered and thrilled even his own group several years later.

But, compared to these commercial recordings and radio transcriptions, Parker's live work with McShann was really something to marvel at, as Gene Ramey has described it:

Bird kept everybody on the stand happy, because he was a wizard at transmitting musical messages to us, which made us fall out laughing. All musicians know certain musical phrases that translate themselves into 'Hello beautiful' or, when a young lady ambles to the powder room, 'I know where you're going'. Well, Bird had an ever-increasing repertoire of these . . . Sometimes on the dance floor, while he was playing, women who were dancing would perform in front of him . . . As soon as his tones became piercing, we were all so accustomed to his reactions that we understood at once what he meant.

He was just as capable of hearing a car horn and not only reproducing the sound but working it into his solo. But it was the instant fusion of this instinctual side of Parker's playing with the utterly logical and technically justifiable advances beyond the developments of Lester Young and Coleman Hawkins that grabbed his colleagues.

After the McShann band made its successful New York debut in January 1942, jazz-minded musicians gravitated to the Savoy

Ballroom to study the saxophonist at close quarters, and a select few such as Sid Catlett and Dizzy Gillespie were allowed to sit in. Gillespie, first introduced to Parker by Buddy Anderson in 1940, had spent the whole day jamming with him at the 'coloured' musicians' union hall in Kansas City (the same building featured in the film *Last of the Blue Devils*); now a leading light of New York's underground avant-garde, he was playing regularly (unpaid) with the house band at Minton's in Harlem which included Thelonious Monk and drummer Kenny Clarke. Charlie naturally played on occasion at this 'laboratory of bebop' and was actually recorded there more than once by amateur sound engineer Jerry Newman, but these documents have yet to be issued publicly. There is available, however, a version of *Cherokee* from this period with the non-union house band at another Harlem night-spot (even more famous at the time, although Charlie had either failed to visit it or failed to make an impact there in 1939), Clarke Monroe's Uptown House. Charlie now found the locals were no longer so daunting but merely something more that he could learn from and absorb: 'I began to listen to that real advanced New York style. At Monroe's . . . I'd listen to trumpet men like Lips Page, Roy [Eldridge], Dizzy and Charlie Shavers, outblowing each other all night long. And Don Byas was there, playing everything there was to be played.'

With Charlie doubling in both the more formalised surroundings of the McShann band and the cut-and-thrust of Harlem jam-sessions, with no time for regular sleep or regular meals but a lot of time devoted to scoring drugs, he was becoming less reliable than for quite some time. *Cherokee* was his special feature number with McShann, but on one occasion he was absent from the Savoy until, half-way through the number, he appeared playing his solo on the dance-floor; during another *Cherokee*, although seated on the bandstand, he fell asleep instead of starting to play. Early on in the New York stay, he had been sacked and reinstated after a brawl with Walter Brown, and once he nearly set his hotel room alight by falling asleep with a lighted cigarette. Finally, when the band visited Detroit, he had to be left behind suffering from inferior heroin or an overdose, or both. Joining the Andy Kirk band in order to play his way back to New York, he became a full-time but ill-paid member of the band at

Monroe's and then, subsidised by the musicians officially employed at Minton's, a supernumary of their band. But, so far, these were virtually the only colleagues who were interested in his welfare.

If Charlie's abundant technique and imagination could have been easily assimilated into the current swing groups, rather than posing an apparent threat to them (and especially to their saxophone players), he might have found steady employment downtown in the small clubs of 52nd Street, with bandleaders he was heard by in Harlem. Instead, in December 1942 he was insinuated into the touring band of Earl Hines, who had expressed interest in him while still with McShann and who had recently been persuaded to hire Dizzy Gillespie also. The largely Chicago-based musicians that populated the band already included two altoists, Goon Gardner and Scoops Carry, so it was agreed that Charlie would play tenor saxophone only, provided Hines would buy one for him. But, except in the eyes of one or two of the band members, he was no longer the leading light he had been with McShann. The featured soloist in the Earl Hines band was Earl Hines, with Charlie just one of several others deserving some solo space each night; his main spot was on a ballad featuring Sarah Vaughan, who joined a month later, and not all the rest of the band's repertoire was as stimulating as Gillespie's contributions like *Down Under, Salt Peanuts* and *Night in Tunisia*.

Unfortunately, no records were made of this transitional band because of the musicians' union ban on recording from August 1942 and, oddly enough, not a single aircheck has yet come to light. But what the eight months with Hines did triumphantly was to cement the relationship between Parker and Gillespie. During occasional weeks when the band was in New York at the Apollo and the two leading modernists were jamming at Minton's every night as well, Charlie put the finishing touches to the synthesis of his Kansas City background and the advanced New York style, a synthesis that was to become known as 'bebop'. In 1980, Gillespie told me that, despite his own important harmonic contributions, 'Charlie Parker, as we all know, was the catalyst. He was the establisher of the style.' And, while the band was on the road, the collaboration between the two continued non-stop.

'We were together all the time, playing in hotel rooms and jamming . . . The guys who pushed dope would be around, but when he wasn't with them, he was with me . . . He might smoke a joint or something, but he would never take off in front of me.' But, when it came to the job with the Hines band, Charlie was often missing performances altogether or nodding off on stage. Earl Hines was impressed by his seeming ability to improvise by sheer reflex action within seconds of being woken up.

In April 1943, as the band finished ten days in Washington, Charlie married for the second time. Gerri Scott, whom he seems to have met a year earlier while with the McShann band, was a nightclub dancer perhaps more in love with the life of showbusiness people than she thought she was with Charlie, while he for his part must have assumed her to be capable of providing money and stability. 'When I met him, all he had was a horn and a habit. He gave me the habit,' she said later. It therefore must have seemed almost logical to Charlie to borrow back her wedding ring from time to time in order to drop hints about marriage with other girls, especially ones who could 'lend' him the money to score a fix for him and his wife. Within eighteen months at most, he and Gerri had separated and, during the 1950s, she served a sentence at the same West Virginia reformatory in which Billie Holiday had been imprisoned.

Chapter Four

By the end of 1943 Parker was, if not yet out of control, spinning slightly out of orbit. He had left the Hines band early in August while they were again in Washington, briefly entertaining the idea of settling down with Gerri in her home town. After working there with Sir Charles Thompson, he was soon to be found back in his own home town, where he worked for Tootie Clarkin with a compatible sextet including Buddy Anderson. And early the next year he was heard of in Chicago, in the bands of first Noble Sissle and then Carroll Dickerson. While in Kansas City, he was surprised to meet the first new altoist to become a member of the Charlie Parker 'school', when 19-year-old Sonny Stitt came through with Tiny Bradshaw's band:

I rushed over and said belligerently, 'Are you Charlie Parker?' He said he was and invited me right then and there to go and jam with him at a place called Chauncey Owenman's. We played for an hour, till the owner came in, and then Bird signalled me with a little flurry of notes to cease so no words would ensue. He said, 'You sure sound like me.'

While he absented himself from New York during the winter of 1943-44, the first bebop group to be booked on 52nd Street had appeared without him. Led by Dizzy Gillespie and bassist Oscar Pettiford – who the previous winter had been keen enough to carry his bass halfway across Chicago during a snowstorm to play in a hotel room with Diz and Bird, and had subsequently rehearsed with them in New York – the group at the Onyx and then the Downbeat included Don Byas (later Budd Johnson) on saxophone and an 18-year-old Max Roach at the drums. Meanwhile, the record ban had come to an end as not only some medium-large companies but a rash of small labels interested in jazz agreed to the union's terms; of course, even the small labels thought in terms of established jazz figures, but there were opportunities for the young beboppers, which Charlie missed. Ironically, when the members of the Gillespie-Pettiford group and others recorded with Coleman Hawkins in February 1944, Gillespie's arrangement of *Disorder at the Border* paid tribute to Parker by using the saxophone riff from *Jumpin' Blues* behind the Gillespie solo and part of the main theme from the same record behind Hawkins. What with Bennie Harris taking the opening phrase of Parker's recorded solo on *Jumpin' Blues* as the start of his tune *Ornithology*, it was as if Charlie was being analysed and anthologised because his in-person contribution could not be relied on.

The person who brought him back into the limelight was Billy Eckstine, a vocalist of increasing popularity but also a fan of the new jazzmen. Accepting the current notion that anybody who was anybody needed his own big-band backing, Eckstine hired Dizzy

Gillespie as his musical director and personally located Charlie to lead the saxophone section. By the time he joined the band in the spring, he had already missed their first record session. However, his by now expected unreliability apart, he was full of enthuiasm for Eckstine's personnel and repertoire, both of which were partial holdovers from the Hines band. But it soon became evident that the uncompromising stance of Gillespie's arrangements, even behind vocals, was creating resistance among provincial audiences. Eckstine recalled that

> Diz made an arrangement of *Max Is Makin' Wax*, which was way up there [fast], featuring him and Bird. You couldn't dance to that, but people would just stand there and watch . . . During the war . . . people weren't ready at that particular time for a concert style of jazz.

During the war also, there was supposed to be less racial disharmony but, when these young musicians acted as uncompromisingly as their music, the lack of servility angered promoters as well as some patrons. So the disillusioned Parker was glad to accept an offer to return to New York as a member of the Ben Webster quintet on 52nd Street. Happily for us, the fact that he also sat in further down The Street at Tondelayo's with ex-Art Tatum guitarist Tiny Grimes led to Charlie being summoned at less than 24 hours' notice for Grimes's September recording date. *I'll Always Love You* provides an example of his work on vocal ballads, which so far had gone unrecorded although a popular feature with the McShann, Hines and Eckstine bands; while, on *Tiny's Tempo* and *Red Cross* (the latter theme by Parker although related to a rhythmic figure created by Sid Catlett and recorded the previous year by Coleman Hawkins as *Mop Mop*), we hear the chord sequences of, respectively, the blues and *I Got Rhythm* which Charlie used for so much of his best work. This session represents his longest exposure on records prior to his own first date and, as with the majority of his subsequent studio work, the issue of alternative versions shows his apparent freedom to build a new solo on each performance combined with the self-discipline to keep improving from one take to the next.

With Grimes, the rhythm playing has a pre-bebop feel and, as on the slightly later records led by Sir Charles Thompson, Red Norvo etc., Charlie's involved but relaxed playing suits the group perfectly well. Attempting to explain the development of his own rhythmic freedom out of the previously accepted swing style, he once said, 'I think that the music of today is a sort of combination of the Midwestern beat and the fast New York tempos.' For his first small-band gig with Gillespie when he too left Eckstine and was booked on the Street, Parker was blessed with his first fully compatible rhythm-section: bassist Curly Russell, no guitar (an important step in the avoidance of rhythmic and harmonic restriction), and two white musicians, Al Haig on piano and a former colleague of Dizzy's and fan of Max Roach on drums, Stan Levey.

The live impact of the first Gillespie-Parker stint at the Three Deuces in late 1944 can only be dimly sensed from their recordings of the following spring. But the perfectly blended and razor-sharp unison playing on up-tempo themes like *Groovin' High, Dizzy Atmosphere, Shaw Nuff* and *Salt Peanuts* exactly mirrors the style of the succeeding solos by both parties, and betokens their growing collaboration during the preceding three years. The importance of the original themes in codifying the new solo styles was realised by all concerned. Oscar Pettiford was aware of Parker the composer in 1943, and Gillespie (who said 'I had been putting down Bird's solos on paper, which is something Bird never had the patience for himself') recalled Parker coming to his apartment in the middle of the night:

From the other room, my wife yelled, 'Throw him out,' and I obediently slammed the door in Bird's face. Parker then took his horn to his mouth and played the tune in the hallway. I grabbed a pencil and paper and took it down from the other side of the door.

Although their closeness at the time makes the collaboration with Gillespie hard to untangle, Parker's other notable themes from this prolific period include *Koko, Anthropology* (a.k.a. *Thriving on a Riff*) and *Confirmation.*

The significance of this first appearance on 52nd. St. must be measured in terms of the Street itself. The basement clubs, some of which had begun life during Prohibition, were the undisputed mecca for all types of small-group jazz. Although they were tiny and their amenities such that people in the music business referred to them casually as 'toilets', they were where the innovations and reputations established in Harlem and around the country were unveiled to New York's white cognoscenti. Once the partnership of Parker and Gillespie had coalesced and the name 'bebop' adhered to it, its recognition by 52nd. St. led to record dates and helped the music to gain its first hard-core followers. Also, the habit of performers on the Street of visiting each other's venues during breaks enabled more conservative players to hear the new style fully-fledged and to react either with interest or, in many cases, with alarm and hostility. Charles Mingus once remarked, without undue exaggeration, that 'The critics tried to stop Bird . . . All the guys on top except Duke Ellington put down Charlie Parker, because they knew they'd have to change what they were doing.' Meanwhile, Gillespie and Parker were seeking to expand their horizons and their audience by appearing in concert twice at Town Hall and by sitting in with Machito's popular Afro-Cuban band; and, as Dizzy told me:

Charlie Parker and I were closely connected with the African Academy of Arts and Research from Nigeria, and we became closely acquainted with some of the Africans that were studying in the United States. And we played benefits all over New York, just with the trumpet and the saxophone and African drums. It was never recorded but, man, we used to get into some *grooves*, with those Africans *dancing* and everything while we're playing.

Apart from a period early in 1945 when Charlie deputised in the Cootie Williams band, he was to be featured at various 52nd St. clubs frequently throughout the year, even when Dizzy went off in mid-1945 to form his first short-lived big-band and was replaced by Don Byas. Now well enough known to be hired as a leader, Charlie was able to employ Dexter Gordon, Bud Powell and the young Miles Davis, whose induction to the big-time had begun when he temporarily replaced an ailing Buddy Anderson in the Eckstine band. Charlie, however, although a veteran of the big-time and a leader in his own right, had been shacking up in Miles's apartment (and doubtless looking after some of his allowance too) until, some time during 1945, he moved into the apartment of Doris Sydnor, one of the many white women who now took an interest in him.

By November, Gillespie was back in New York and using

Charlie in his group again, which is how Dizzy came to replace Bud Powell on piano for much of Parker's benchmark recording date that same month. Despite the confusion over availability of pianists (detailed in the notes to the Savoy reissue set) and the saxophone repairs in mid-session which were the cause of two bonus warm-up tracks being recorded, Parker was in complete command musically. On his two blues pieces, the traditional-sounding *Now's the Time* and the rhythmically involved *Billie's Bounce* (composed on the day of the recording), he shows how far he has travelled since *Hootie Blues*. Spurred on by the drums of Max Roach *Koko*, based like *Warming Up a Riff* on *Cherokee*, takes some of his favourite ideas sketched on the 1942 Monroe's version a stage further and, for the first time on a commercial record, sets down Parker's new standards for combined invention and execution at high speed – standards which have yet to be surpassed nearly 40 years later.

Despite Parker's brilliance on this session, his apparent nihilism and irresponsibility were no secret to Gillespie. So, when the quintet set out for the West Coast in December, it was augmented by Milt Jackson to share the solo load during Charlie's anticipated absences. He lived up to expectations so well that, after a week, the nightclub owner insisted on hiring another saxist, Lucky Thompson, to make up the numbers to six on a regular basis. Later Charlie would rationalise his frequent defections by referring to the uncomprehending response of the Hollywood crowd who patronised Billy Berg's, but there was overwhelming acceptance from the local musicians, especially though not exclusively the black musicians. There was interest from the media too with approaches to make records for Dial, live broadcasts from the club every night for two weeks, and guest appearances on both the Rudy Vallee show(!) and the Armed Forces Radio Service 'Jubilee' series. The latter's producer Jimmy Lyons, who claimed to have recommended the band to Billy Berg in the first place, wrote about their guest spot:

> They were late. All the studio musicians were already on risers on the stage. And we had a live audience, composed of injured guys from the hospital. Dizzy turned and kicked off the first tune on the roster with his heel, *Hot House.* The place went up in flames. The studio guys just threw their instruments up in

the air. They started laughing and holding onto themselves, watching these strange youngsters playing their funny music. Another producer destined for fame, Norman Granz, introduced Parker and Gillespie to another enthusiastic non-nightclub audience at one of his Jazz At The Philharmonic concerts. When issued on records, Charlie's solo on the pre-bebop style *Lady Be Good*, although typical rather than outstanding, drew attention to the similarities and differences between him and the now detached and withdrawn Lester Young. But it was during the extended collaboration at Berg's that similarities and differences between Charlie and Dizzy became evident as never before. The two most advanced soloists in the country at the time, Dizzy was training for the marathon while his colleague was the man on the flying trapeze. Observing Charlie to be such a profligate spendthrift, musically as much as financially, Dizzy realised he himself wasn't built that way and became aware of the value of organisation, both of his own playing and of his bands. Trumpeter Howard McGhee, an ardent admirer of both men, once told me pensively:

> I think Charlie Parker was the most outspoken [musically] out of the whole group, because sometimes he used to make Dizzy sound like a toy. Because he had an unlimited amount of ideas. He's the only man I know who had a photographic mind in music.

And yet, though temperamentally geared to living (and playing) for the moment, such a mind was not only organised but also *capable* of conscious organisation. The famous break on his March 1946 record of *Night in Tunisia*, which has been hailed as a great spontaneous invention, is repeated note for note on all the takes recorded that day; and, what is more, most of the live versions extant find Parker repeating the majority of the same phrase, and varying or even improving the overall outline only slightly.

By this time, however, disorganisation was the keynote of Charlie's lifestyle. He might well have been recording *Night in Tunisia* five weeks earlier in New York with Dizzy, had he not cashed in his airline ticket before he was due to return with the rest of the band. Shortly after his own record session, at which a new *I Got Rhythm* tune had been created in the studio, its dedicatee *Moose the Mooche* (the local heroin connection) had been imprisoned and Charlie was using port, the wino's consolation, and then whisky and benzedrine as an ineffectual substitute. Although doing fairly regular club dates with Howard McGhee and others, and further concerts for Norman Granz, he was panicked by the realisation that he could no longer do without hard drugs.

His eventual breakdown is all too well documented due to the coincidence of a recording session held on July 29, 1946. No longer in a position to play even by reflex action, Parker can be heard struggling valiantly to execute simple phrases and, with a supreme effort of will, turning the ballad *Lover Man* into an almost coherent solo. Coming a mere eight months after *Koko*, this sounds like the dying words of someone wounded in battle. After his contribution to the session, he succeeded in setting his hotel room on fire, was clubbed and arrested by the local police, and finally committed to the state mental hospital at Camarillo. Charlie was out of orbit, out of control, and now out of circulation for the next six months.

Chapter Five

When Charlie emerged from Camarillo in February 1947, he was in good health for the first time in ten years. After the rehabilitation effected by regular meals and an absence of drugs and alcohol (and the cure of a bout of syphilis), he had decided to treat his enforced stay as a welcome rest from the pressures of following his chosen profession. Psychologically, he was well-balanced enough, or at least street-wise enough, to avoid giving the doctors any justification for tampering with his personality. If they had really probed beneath its surface equanimity, they would have discovered not only all the normal well-founded resentments of the minority members of an aggressively white society, but an awareness of the burdens of a revolutionary artist. And in particular his feelings about California ('Nobody understood our kind of music. They *hated* it,' he said later) probably translated into a generalisation that the supposedly hip audiences were just as bad as the police and the doctors. In fact, Charlie would have been quite capable of alleging that he was locked up *because* he played music that 'nobody' understood.

By the end of his six months, however, Charlie was eager to get back to playing and, despite the working conditions which it entailed, convinced that he could evade the possibility of re-addiction. And, while waiting for employment to be arranged so that he and Doris (who had joined him on the Coast) could return to New York, he was happy to play with Howard McGhee's band and at various jam-sessions. Even more than before his hospitalisation, all manner of musicians wanted to sit in with him and get the 'word from the Bird'. 'Who didn't that was searching for new techniques on their instruments?' said Roy Porter, the superior drummer who had been on the 1946 recordings; for Charlie's influence was now speading like wildfire, principally through records, and creating disciples not only on the alto (beginning with Sonny Stitt, Sonny Criss, Jimmy Heath and Art Pepper) but on everything else as well. Only Louis Armstrong in the 1920s had caused such a tidal change in the way the music was played.

Parker's last two West Coast record dates included a homogeneous septet session, for which his one new theme – written in a taxi on the way to the rehearsal – was a complex blues called *Relaxin' at Camarillo*. On the day of recording, his playing appeared to reflect the title, even though he was badly hung-over and had slept the night in a bathtub following a row with Doris. The relaxation was even more obvious the previous week, on one of Charlie's few saxophone-and-rhythm-only recordings. The accompaniment of the Erroll Garner trio with Doc West on drums, previously heard on the Tiny Grimes date, imparts a pre-bebop feel which throws into greater relief the soaring lines of the alto on *Cool Blues* and especially *Bird's Nest*. At the same time his desire to feature one of the sitting-in breed, an inferior imitator of Billy Eckstine called Earl Coleman, resulted in Charlie's ballad playing behind the vocal on *Dark Shadows* making it his most commercially successful record so far.

When Charlie and Doris arrived back in New York after an Easter weekend gig in Chicago, he appeared as a guest soloist with Dizzy Gillespie's thriving new big-band, and then set about assembling the quintet which was to be his regular working group for the next few years. To the essential ingredient of Max Roach on drums, he added Miles Davis, bassist Tommy Potter (who had first worked with him in the Washington band) and, on the May 1947 record session, Bud Powell. A certain unresolved tension in this session, which begat *Cheryl* and *Chasing the Bird*, may have caused the choice of pianist Duke Jordan to join the group when it began a long stint at the Three Deuces on 52nd St. When three months later the 21-year-old Davis was awarded his first recording under his own name (with Parker playing tenor for the first time on disc), he used Gillespie's pianist and arranger John Lewis, who often sat in with the Parker group while Dizzy was at the Downbeat. Duke Jordan noted that

> [Miles] wanted Bird to substitute John for me in the group. But Bird silenced him quietly and firmly saying that he chose the guys and Miles could form his own outfit if anything displeased him. That was all that was heard from Miles.

Such quiet confidence in his own choice of musical direction, as opposed to sometimes arbitary authoritarianism, was relatively unusual in Charlie. The man Ross Russell described as a 'charismatic egomaniac' habitually relied on these qualities to carry him through any situation, and he was not used to being denied. Although now fronting his own group regularly, it was said that no one would ever accuse Charlie of being a bandleader – which is something in which Gillespie, and very soon Miles Davis also, were to become extremely skilled. But, whereas the relationship of Gillespie with Parker was one of equality, their different strengths complementing each other, Davis was very much the junior partner with Charlie. Still refining his fairly clumsy technique and searching for his personal style, he said, 'Bird used to make me play. He used to lead me up on the bandstand. I used to quit every night. The tempos were so fast, the challenge so great. I used to ask, "What do you need me for?" ' Again, it says much for Charlie's sense of direction at this stage that he recognised Miles's potential and persevered with him despite criticism of his work from others.

Charlie, of course, continued to make guest appearances away from his own quintet, including 'battles of the bands' between a 'modern' group and a traditional New Orleans-style band, broadcast on the Mutual Network. (One of these provoked a convincing Parker-Gillespie adaptation of *Tiger Rag*, incorporating the secondary theme of *Dizzy Atmosphere!*) There was another set with Gillespie during the first bebop concert to be held at Carnegie Hall, shared by Ella Fitzgerald and Gillespie's own band, the recording of which preserves a stunning example of Charlie's ability to perform under less than favourable circumstances. Co-producer Teddy Reig recalled that, as before the *Relaxin'* date, Charlie was asleep in the bath:

> We went to his room [at the Dewey Square Hotel] and broke down the bathroom door. We got him out of the tub, dried him, dressed him, got him in a cab, stuck the horn in his hands, and pushed from the wings onto the stage. The result, which was recorded, . . . is unbelievable in its speed, ideas, and artistry.

It seems that Charlie was drinking heavily, at times excessively, to counteract the desire for other drugs. Duke Jordan reported an instance in Chicago in November 1947 of him becoming incapable of playing due to alcohol, whereas heroin works in an opposite way so that the addict becomes dependent on it to function normally and it is only the withdrawal of the drug which produces unpleasant physical symptoms. Yet Ross Russell, not only Charlie's biographer but at this stage still his record producer, observed him using heroin to get 'up' for a studio session in October that year. It may be that his untypical physiology again enabled him to take the drug from time to time without actually becoming re-addicted, for Jordan corroborated Charlie's continued involvement:

> Wherever we would be, the pushers were with us. The grapevine, as far as drugs is concerned, is very quick, very swift; and as soon as Bird hit town, someone would contact him. 'I know where something real good is,' they would say, sometimes calling the hotel at five or six in the morning, and Bird would go with them. As years went by, Bird started

cooling. He went to a doctor in 1948 and was told he had about six months to live unless he took a complete rest for a few years, which he never did.

It has to be mentioned, too, that despite this diagnosis Charlie's notoriety had by now become almost as influential as his music, especially in the eyes of players who persuaded themselves that his apparently superhuman musical ability was somehow the result of using heroin. A full list of those concerned would be too depressingly long for the scope of this book but, for instance, all four altoists mentioned on page 00 were to have a serious addiction problem which interrupted their careers. Of course, the people who made available the heroin are finally more to be blamed, but unfortunately Parker's association gave it an air of desirability, no matter what the consequences.

Nevertheless, it was at this period that Charlie made what are not only his finest studio recordings but some of the greatest in the history of jazz. Between October 1947 and September 1948, the quintet took part in six sessions (once augmented by trombonist J.J. Johnson) and the resultant series of performances has the kind of stylistic perfection for which there are very few possible comparisons. Louis Armstrong's Hot Fives, the 1937-8 Count Basies, the 1940-1 Ellingtons, the Miles Davis 1955-6 quintet, the Ornette Coleman 1959-60 quartet and John Coltrane's 1960 quartet virtually complete the list – and, already by the time of the last three groups, recording on tape had minimised some of the rigid distinctions between studio and live performance which still applied in Parker's day. The 30 titles from these sessions, each intended originally for issue in a single version, have the homogeneity and unity of purpose typical of a regular working group at its peak, but also display a rewarding variety both of texture and of material. Some of the latter is discussed in more detail in Chapter 8 but it is worth noting here that, not counting 'themeless' improvisations and those based on standard songs, there are no fewer than 20 new Parker 'originals' (*Crazeology*, a.k.a. *Little Benny* or *Bud's Bubble*, was a mid-1940s creation by Benny Harris). Along with some of the Gillespie tunes, and a few Monk and Tadd Dameron items, they constitute the most impressive written work of the bebop era. And yet, according to Tommy Potter, 'On recording dates he could compose right on the spot. The A. & R. man would be griping, wanting us to begin. Charlie would say, "It'll just take a minute," and he'd write out eight bars, usually just for the trumpet. He could transpose it for his alto without a score.'

The contribution of the other players should not be underestimated, especially Miles Davis who proceeded undeterred to define his role as an emotional counterweight, but the most impressive aspect of these records is Charlie's authoritative yet mellow solo work. This shows particularly on the numbers without an ensemble theme-statement where, after the briefest of introductions, he establishes the mood with classic composure; this is equally true of the ultra-fast *Merry-Go-Round*, *Klaunstance* (based on *The Way You Look Tonight*) and *Bird Gets the Worm* (*Lover Come Back to Me*) as it is of the ballads such as *Bird of Paradise* (*All the Things You Are*) and *Embraceable You*. Most notable in this category is the slow blues masterpiece, *Parker's Mood*, where with no trumpet to act as a foil, and even an inappropriately twee piano solo failing to distract, the alto digs down to the roots of black music while majestically updating its language. 'Themeless' in the sense that there is no pre-composed blues tune (despite the Armstrong-like opening and closing fanfare), it is pure vocal melody – involved yet basic, finely-sculptured but raw, eminently singable even before the addition of King Pleasure's evocative lyrics some five years later.

Interestingly, the live recordings from the first half of 1948 (at the Three Deuces and the Onyx) tend to corroborate Tommy Potter's statement, insofar as very little of the new original repertoire created in the studio is used in public. *Scrapple from the Apple* became popular with other musicians but, in contrast to Gillespie who was using masses of new material in his live performances and broadcasts, Charlie's performing repertoire at this period consisted mostly of standard songs or the bebop classics of a few years earlier such as *Night in Tunisia*, *Dizzy Atmosphere* and *Shaw Nuff*. This also corroborates Miles Davis's comment that Parker never rehearsed with the quintet: 'He never did talk about music. I always even had to show Duke Jordan, the pianist in the band, the chords.' Charlie as a bandleader managed to create other problems for his sidemen, often concerning money. Now he was in a position to withhold their salaries arbitrarily or even, as Max Roach said,

> Because of some of his irresponsible acts, the rest of the men would be docked or the owner would try to get out of paying the rest of us anything. I would start beefing to Bird, 'I was here all night and working for you.' I would chide him about his responsibilities as leader.

Some of the more drastic actions which Max complained about included Charlie throwing his saxophone out of an upper-floor window, and taking the colloquial description of a nightclub as a 'toilet' literally by peeing on the floor. In the face of such suicidal provocation, both Miles and Max resigned from the band at the Onyx in mid-summer 1948, although the separation was by no means final. One of the appearances they obtained under Miles's name included Parker in the front-line, and he guested with Miles and Max on the opening night of Miles's nine-piece band at the Royal Roost. And, when Charlie himself took the quintet into the Roost in December for a long stay, both Davis and Roach rejoined — Miles for a couple of weeks, Max for several months.

What Charlie had been doing during the autumn was to capitalise on his growing reputation, and at the same time earn what was then very generous payment, by taking part in one of the first extended tours by Norman Granz's Jazz At The Philharmonic concert package with Howard McGhee, Coleman Hawkins and others. And, while on the West Coast for this tour, he took Doris down to Tijuana and got married for the third time. Charlie had been told by the doctor that, while he may have been cooling on the drugs front, his alcohol consumption had given him a serious ulcer condition. This may have influenced his sudden decision to formalise the three-year relationship with Doris, although she apparently felt they were already drifting apart: 'I really had no strong desire for marriage, but Charlie was going through a jealousy period, a romantically insecure stage with me; so I said yes.' As a sort of wedding present and in recognition of the fact that Charlie was beginning to 'make it', his booking agent Billy Shaw decided that Charlie should have his own Cadillac ('The one he was gonna get rid of, anyway, you know', in the words of Budd Johnson). But, according to Doris Parker, the money to pay for it came from Charlie's earnings with the agency, and this is certainly possible since his period of less frequent drug use coincided with a considerable increase in income.

Aware that some of the comparative squares who saw him in concert did so because of his junkie status, he frequently admonished both musicians and fans against the fascination of stimulants:

> Any musician who says he is playing better either on tea, the needle, or when he is juiced, is a plain, straight liar. When I get too much to drink, I can't even finger well, let alone play decent ideas. And, in the days when I was on the stuff, I may have *thought* I was playing better, but listening to some of the records now, I know I wasn't.

While he never forgave Ross Russell for issuing the *Lover Man* session, it is just as well he was unaware that technology, through wire and then tape machines, was beginning to enable the unauthorised recording of apparently ephemeral live appearances and broadcasts. The posthumous release of such material has given us, as well as some merely indifferent performances, dazzling moments like the 1947 Carnegie Hall concert. And the fifteen Royal Roost broadcasts of 1948-9, of which a comprehensive issue is still awaited although several tracks have been available for twenty years, provide new insights into Parker's playing barely hinted at in his studio work, such as the casual, open-ended invention of the February 12 *Barbados*. But the January 29 version of *Groovin' High*, never publicly released, includes a single incoherent phrase from Charlie before he lapses into silence (and, according to announcer Symphony Sid's recollection, sleep) for the rest of the broadcast. Four weeks later, *Night in Tunisia* finds him audibly losing his nerve during the famous alto break, and sounding every bit as uncoordinated as on the *Lover Man* session.

Chapter Six

By the start of 1949 the outlook for Charlie did not seem bright. He knew that he was ignoring the doctor's advice, and he knew that he was sometimes not performing to the best of his ability. But this was at least partly related to the conditions under which he was obliged to perform; after his return from the Coast, he had expressed satisfaction that at least in New York bebop had achieved some popularity with younger listeners, and this feeling was undoubtedly reinforced by touring the nation's concert halls with Jazz At The Philharmonic. Before this, however, Duke Jordan had observed that

> Bird knew the limitations of his success and felt annoyed that he was confined to just playing nightclubs. He was also bugged by the fact that, being a Negro, he could go just so far and no farther. Once he finished a set to great acclaim, ducked out, and went quietly to a bar around the corner on Sixth Avenue between 51st and 52nd Street, called McGuire's. The paradox of his life was brought into focus when the bartender asked what he wanted and addressed him as a 'nigger'. Parker vaulted over the bar to teach the fellow manners.

One sharp ray of sunlight during the stay at the Roost was the invitation for the quintet (now including trumpeter Kenny Dorham, and Al Haig in place of Jordan) to the second Paris Jazz Fair. Howard McGhee's group had been to the festival the previous year when Dizzy's big band also appeared in France, while Don Byas and Kenny Clarke had gone so far as to settle there. It was widely believed to be a country without any racial prejudice, and certainly the longevity of jazz appreciation there had created an awareness that all the historically significant contributions had been made by black musicians. So it was hardly surprising that the festival's bebop representatives – the Parker group and the Tadd Dameron/Miles Davis quintet – were lionised just as much as the other guest soloists, Sidney Bechet (who also ended up staying on in France) and Hot Lips Page. The overwhelming effect of their acceptance was recalled by Tommy Potter: 'The reception in France was lavish. Autograph-signing parties in record shops and lots of press coverage topped by a press party in Bird's hotel room.'

While in Paris, Charlie was delighted to be introduced to the renowned 'classical' saxophonist Marcel Mule, and it may be during the period following his European trip that he actually took saxophone *lessons* with the noted teacher Henry Lindeman – presumably with a view to improving his tone production rather than his already awesome facility! An interview done in the summer of 1949 by John S. Wilson and Mike Levin found Charlie saying that:

> For the future, he'd like to go to the Academy of Music in Paris for a couple of years, then relax for a while and then write . . . Ideally, he'd like to spend six months a year in France and six months here. 'You've got to do it that way,' he explains. 'You've got to be here for the commercial things and in France for relaxing facilities.'

Whether or not Charlie would ever have had the discipline to 'write' in a premeditated way, he had since settling in New York become deeply interested in European music. His photographic mind enabled him to incorporate specific quotations from Chopin or Debussy into an improvised solo (probably only when there was someone in the audience who would understand the reference), and in various interviews he mentioned his liking for Bach, Beethoven, Bartok and Shostakovitch, often naming particular works such as Milhaud's *Protée* or Schoenberg's *Pierrot Lunaire*. Teddy Reig mentioned Charlie borrowing his classical records: 'I had three copies of the *Concertino da Camera for Saxophone and Orchestra* [by Ibert] and Bird got everyone.' And Charles Mingus, who described Parker improvising along with a Stravinsky piece, attempted a similar combination on his recording of *The Chill of Death*, a work Charlie admired as evidence that Mingus was 'a good writer'.

Now that Charlie's association with Norman Granz had led to signing with Mercury Records, to whom Granz was leasing his productions, such large-scale efforts seemed more possible. But, unfortunately, the results were musically disappointing. Charlie's first studio recording for Granz in 1948 was a contribution to a special album project called *The Jazz Scene*, featuring Duke Ellington, Lester Young, Coleman Hawkins and others: on *Repetition*, his improvisation was dubbed over the second half of a tedious, Stan Kenton-style big-band-with-strings piece by Neal Hefti (who later went on to write such gems as *Girl Talk* and *Batman* but, according to Buster Smith, also used to hang around the Kansas City jam-sessions with Charlie when he too was a teenager). For the same album, with just a rhythm section, Charlie cut his longest solo ever on a commercial record, an improvisation on *Topsy* called *The Bird* and containing a fund of ideas, marred only by an apparent uncertainty as to just how long the recording would run.

But the idea of doing a whole album (in those days, this meant a group of singles sold together and often available separately as well) featuring Parker with strings was met with immediate enthusiasm by both Granz as his recording manager and Billy Shaw. As Shaw and doubtless Charlie were aware, Dizzy had already recorded with strings on the West Coast in 1946, only to have the releases blocked by the publisher concerned. Not only did the musical texture appeal to Charlie, but it would be a way to capitalise on the popularity of his ballad improvisations, only recently heard for the first time on record without the accompaniment of vocalists, in *Embraceable You* and others. The way the album turned out, however, it was definitely one of 'the commercial things' and not necessarily in the way that Charlie intended. Despite his lyrical solo on *Just Friends* with its beautifully integrated quotation from *My Man* in the last half-chorus, this is the only improvisation longer than 16 bars and elsewhere his decorative ideas are deliberately reined in, often cut off in mid-phrase. And though the unashamedly schmaltzy arrangements by former Alec Wilder sideman Jimmy Carroll are fairly inoffensive, the really dispiriting thing is the way the piano solos and the rhythm section slot into a businessman's bounce at every opportunity. There must have been a knowing irony in Charlie's telephone call to his mother, 'Mama, I'm going to the top, my name's going to be in lights,' and indeed, on the strength of his statement of the melodies, *April in Paris* and *Just Friends* became his best-selling records ever.

It was not before time that Charlie should look for a more prestigious outlet than his continual appearances in nightclubs, especially since the lively and fraternal scene which had once been 52nd St. was completely dead by the end of 1949. With the

41

exception of the Three Deuces where the quintet played that autumn after touring the country, the clubs on the Street had turned to striptease and the introduction of jazz at the Royal Roost which was on Broadway had signalled the music's move to more big-time clubs such as the short-lived Bop City, which also featured the quintet in late 1949. But the culmination of this development was the opening on December 15 of the new club which flew the flag of jazz for a decade and a half and which was named, with specific reference to Charlie as a symbol of quality, Birdland. Naturally, he was one of the opening attractions together with Lester Young, Hot Lips Page and Lennie Tristano, and his group for this engagement, with trumpeter Red Rodney and drummer Roy Haynes replacing Dorham and Roach, was also on hand to take part in Symphony Sid's Xmas Eve concert at Carnegie Hall, which was recorded. Further concert presentations early in the New Year with Jazz At The Phil now incorporated the entire quintet and not just Charlie as a soloist, and it must have been during this tour that he recorded three numbers for a Norman Granz film. Two of the pieces, one featuring Charlie with Coleman Hawkins, were issued years later although for some reason a completed film was never released. Nevertheless, the silent footage of Charlie miming to one of these numbers has been made available and been used in various compilations.

On their return to New York, Charlie rehearsed his role as star soloist with a 27-piece band led by ex-Kenton arranger Gene Roland, which unfortunately never obtained any bookings, and the quintet went into another plush nightclub which had not previously taken any interest in bebop, the downtown Cafe Society. The plan had been originally for this to be Charlie's first live engagement with strings and, sartorial elegance never having been his strong point, the occasion was marked by the acquisition of an all-white suit. Unfortunately, the status symbol of the string section had to be postponed, as the white-suited Charlie mention in his on-stage announcements (all delivered in a smooth-talking 1950-disc-jockey style: 'And now for your listening entertainment pleasure, we bring you . . .'). During this period of relative success Doris Parker, despite priding herself on keeping Charlie straight, at least financially, had begun to take a back seat emotionally and eventually went home to her mother.

> I was nervous and bothered by low blood pressure and anaemia. I just couldn't take the anxiety of wondering where he was the nights he came home very late or not at all. Visions of him hospitalised or in jail would come into my mind . . . When we broke up, I was very sick, and Charlie never sent me a penny. I had to depend on my family for help.

In July 1950 Charlie consolidated a relationship which had restarted several months earlier, and moved in with Chan Richardson and her three-year-old daughter Kim (who now sings professionally under the name of Kim Parker).

During this period, two all-star sessions took place which both deserve mention. The new Norman Granz recording reunited Charlie with Dizzy Gillespie, for the last time in a studio, and Thelonious Monk, whose only studio session with Charlie this was. As it happens, although it is a joy to hear his accompaniments Monk was allowed little space by the producer, and the choice of Buddy Rich in order to minimise the rhythmic intricacies detracts from the group sound, if not the work of Parker and Gillespie individually. But a special one-off evening later the same month at Birdland was a different matter altogether, for the group that Charlie fronted was so evenly matched that the participants (including Bud Powell, Art Blakey and trumpeter Fats Navarro) seemed determined to outdo each other in excellence. Of Charlie's own work, the mobile yet serene extended solo and the series of alto and trumpet exchanges on *The Street Beat*, as well as his new ideas on *Ornithology* and *Embraceable You*, are outstanding. Immediately afterwards, Birdland also saw the start of several weeks of live performances with the regular rhythm-section plus a string quintet, oboe and harp, to coincide with the recording of a second album. Already at Cafe Society, Charlie had been plugging the first strings album heavily, and the popularity of the concept enabled the new group to appear at Carnegie Hall and Harlem's Apollo Theatre, with the rhythm-section being shared by Stan Getz.

There were subsequent fortnights in Philadelphia and Chicago (where Charlie's unreliability led to a penalty clause in his contract), and then Al Haig, the only other soloist apart from Charlie within the confines of the string arrangements, left the group. Pending further group engagements, Charlie was made available as a single artist to work with local rhythm-sections, as he had done occasionally in the past. The most rewarding result of this was the second brief trip to Europe in November 1950. The reception during the week in Scandinavia was enthusiastic and knowledgeable, and Charlie was particularly impressed to find that Sweden's budding beboppers were on the whole more competent than the Europeans he had heard the previous year. Doubtless he was also looking forward to his scheduled appearance in Paris but, between his arrival there and the date of the concert, he became so overwhelmed by gifts of free drugs and a wide variety of alcohol that he ended up spending his advance payment on an urgent flight back to New York. Ironically, a little over eight years later, Lester Young was to take a similar uncomfortable journey, as he flew home from Paris to die. In Charlie's case, his peptic ulcers merely put him in hospital for several weeks and made him think seriously about mending his ways: 'The doctor told me if I don't quit drinking, I'll die. I've had my last drink.'

Inevitably, this resolution had already been broken long before he went back to work on a series of engagements with the strings. But the belief that his physical constitution was after all superhuman receives considerable support from broadcasts during the three weeks at Birdland during March and April 1951, especially the one in which he was joined by Bud Powell and Dizzy Gillespie. The opening *Blue 'n Boogie*, with its ensemble riffs presumably deriving from a Gillespie arrangement for Earl Hines or Eckstine, sets the tone for a sparkling 25 minutes which put in the shade all the other quintet performances of the period, except for the previous year's Parker-Powell-Navarro date. And a jam-session a fortnight later with Wardell Gray, though more uneven overall, is distinguished by Charlie's nine consecutive choruses (lasting nearly five minutes (on *Scrapple from the Apple*. Taking into account the more inhibiting nature of recording studios, there are also bright moments in the reunion date with Miles Davis (particularly the themeless *K.C. Blues*) and the only studio session with Red Rodney: from the latter, *Si Si, Back Home Blues* and *Blues for Alice* each refer to a descending chord-sequence first outlined in *Confirmation* but which was

A musical home in the Jay McShann Band: Charlie (third from left) looks down at pianist McShann, Walter Brown is next to him (second from left), Little John Jackson is front and centre, while Gus Johnson and Gene Ramey are second from right and far right respectively.)

45

A mid-1940s publicity shot.

A break in the recording studio.

The Charlie Parker Quintet: Tommy Potter (bass), Miles Davis (trumpet), the shoulder of pianist Duke Jordan and, half-hidden behind Charlie, drummer Max Roach.

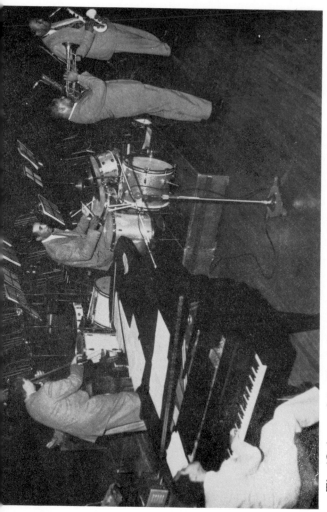

The 'Quintet of the Year': Bud Powell (piano), Charles Mingus (bass), Max Roach, Dizzy Gillespie and Charlie at Massey Hall, Toronto.

Birdland opens with a jam-session of Kansas City stars, Lester Young (tenor), Hot Lips Page (trumpet) and Charlie.

Charlie jamming with the expatriate all-stars, Sidney Bechet (soprano) and Don Byas (tenor), during the finale of the Paris Jazz Fair.

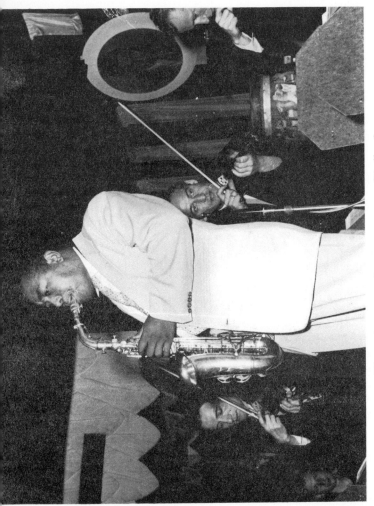

The strings come home to roost at Birdland.

fashionably referred to in the 1950s as 'the Swedish blues'.

There were also many bright moments in Charlie's new home life, including the birth on July 17 of a daughter named Pree. But there were problems too. The lengthy tour with the strings had underlined the anti-improvisation nature of the scores and had often necessitated using local players to read the parts, while the 'novelty' appeal of the group led to them being booked opposite rhythm-&-blues acts such as Ivory Joe Hunter. Furthermore, Charlie's guest spot at Birdland in June with Machito's band, on whose new album he also played briefly, marked his last New York club appearance for 15 months, because the State Liquor Authority which used to license premises selling alcohol also then had the power of licensing all performers in such premises: hence the all-important 'cabaret card' could be withdrawn from anyone convicted (or even suspected) of unlawful behaviour, and this is exactly what happened to Charlie. As a result, Billy Shaw sent him out to play guest spots on a tour with Woody Herman in the Midwest and possibly the West Coast, but he began missing dates and, by the time he was due in Chicago in September, the musicians' union (which had its national stronghold in that city) was on to him with a telegram saying, 'Your agency tells me they cannot locate you. You are directed to contact your agency immediately and play the engagement mentioned above.' Their subsequent investigation of his 'activities' seemingly only managed to turn up a fine owing to the Los Angeles branch from some years before, but this harassment from the union and the events leading up to it forced Billy Shaw to carry out one of his frequent threats not to seek further bookings.

At a loose end professionally, Charlie accompanied his regular pianist of the last few months, Walter Bishop, to a Miles Davis record session in October and found that his former protege was now struggling with his own heroin habit. To add a further touch of irony, Charlie once again won the *Down Beat* readers' poll in December, which resulted in the otherwise unemployed altoist making his only television appearance to have been preserved on film. Around the end of the year, possibly coinciding with the news that Chan was pregnant again, Charlie went back briefly to Kansas City to visit his mother and to 'rest', and as usual he immediately ran through whatever money his mother had put by

('I always had $150 to $200 around the house for his emergencies'). Fifteen months earlier in Detroit, he had been picked up by the FBI for non-payment of alimony, but this particular trip very nearly ended his long-standing record of never being arrested while in possession of drugs. Charlie's mother recalled a redheaded girl who 'pushed dope, and he had met her through one of those numbers on a match cover people were always slipping him'. According to Tootie Clarkin, 'We got word somehow that she was trying to frame him on a narcotics charge for the government. He only had time to play eight bars of *How High the Moon* when we motioned him off the bandstand and helped him to skip town.'

Chapter Seven

Back in New York, no agent had come forward to fill Billy Shaw's shoes, and the only live appearances of the next few months were arranged by friends, with local bands at out-of-town venues such as the Times Square Club in Rochester and the Silver Saddle in Newark. Norman Granz helped out with a batch of record dates which provided some income but little musical stimulus. The big-band and the big-band-plus-strings sessions were doubtless thought to be image-boosting, but potentially more interesting was Charlie's second session with Latin-American percussion. Unlike the extremely restrictive arrangements commissioned for the larger ensembles, this combination could have formed the basis of a rewarding regular group. The interest in Latin music shown by the bop pioneers in the mid-1940s, and the references in several of the classic Parker quintet records, point to a compatibility never fully explored until the 1970s. Charlie was one of the few soloists, along with Gillespie, who could adopt yet still dominate a Latin-American accompaniment and, though less 'up-market' than the strings, such a partnership if pursued in depth might have ensured a more lasting popularity, as well as a more stimulating musical environment.

In late May, Billy Shaw came back into the picture and sent Charlie to the West Coast for several weeks to work as a single with local groups at the Tiffany in Los Angeles and the Say When in San Francisco. But, after an exciting blow with popular tenorman Flip Phillips at the San Francisco club, he managed to get himself fired for speaking his mind about the clubowner. Idle for a week, he sat in with Buddy DeFranco's rhythm section including Art Blakey and, according to Jerome Richardson,

> He was very drunk but he was persuaded to go up on the stand and play . . . 'Anything you want to play', Parker muttered. Blakey said '*52nd Street Theme*' and with that he started a rhythm at a murderously fast tempo. Bird was all tied up. False starts, uncoordinated fingering. He stopped. 'Give me an hour, I'll be back.' No one knows how he did it, but in one hour, he returned cold, deadly sober.

During this period, he also took part in the first studio-recorded jam-session produced by Norman Granz, who not only had tenor saxophonists Phillips and Ben Webster under contract but all three undisputed giants of the alto, Johnny Hodges, Benny Carter and Charlie. No doubt put on his mettle by the company he was in, Charlie played with a brilliant combination of relaxation and invention and, on the famous *Funky Blues*, he can be seen to incorporate both the blues-based power of Hodges and Carter's graceful lyricism with the stylistic innovation that was all his own. Crucial to this session was the new-found freedom of long-play recording, but this freedom was never seriously applied to any of Charlie's own dates, as it would have been had he lived just a couple of years longer.

Finally, around the time that Chan gave birth to their second child Baird on August 10, the Shaw agency persuaded the Liquor Authority to reconsider their decision and, as a result, during the next year Charlie did several separate weeks at New York clubs, most frequently Birdland. For other appearances, he was quite willing to provide a reconstituted string group, a quintet hand-picked (or thrown together) for the occasion, or just his alto saxophone and his charisma. The accompaniments provided on his solo gigs in Chicago, St. Louis (with former Jay McShann colleague Jimmy Forrest), Washington, Boston, Montreal and elsewhere varied considerably as to format and competence, judging from the evidence of live recordings. Having no regular group of his own any more, Charlie was still on the flying trapeze, but now without a safety net; he once said, 'I need a good rhythm section like old people need soft shoes.' As to choice of repertoire, a few of his tunes such as *Now's the Time* and *Scrapple* were known to most musicians who had any pretensions to sharing a bandstand with him and, for the rest, it was a mild form of challenge to play anything the locals could suggest – even their own original arrangements – and still outshine them. The most striking example so far available of this ability is the Washington concert with 'The Orchestra' where, with no rehearsal whatsoever, he fits himself in, over and under the big-band scores of *Willis, Roundhouse* and others as if they had been written expressly for him.

The success of such ventures may be what prompted Billy Shaw to book a week at the Apollo Theatre in April 1953 with a specially assembled 17-piece band, presumably playing arrangements from the 1952 record dates. Even more expensive than the strings, and probably less well rehearsed, this idea was not repeated. What Charlie had on his mind at this period was seemingly more ambitious:

I'd like to do a session with five or six woodwinds, a harp, a choral group, and full rhythm section. Something on the line of Hindemith's *Kleine Kammermusik*. Not a copy or anything like that. I don't want ever to copy. But that sort of thing.

However, even with such an intelligent arranger as Gil Evans, who was then trying hard to make it in the commercial music world, the woodwinds-and-choir record date in May was disappointing. The amount of effort spent in achieving a sound balance and a passable performance resulted in only three tunes being completed rather than the usual four or more, and Norman Granz eventually abandoned the session rather than pay for overtime.

It must have been about this time that the Shaw Agency finally abandoned Charlie too, no doubt causing the first temporary rift between Charlie and Chan. The early morning of May 18 (immediately after returning from a visit to Canada, and, presumably, spending the proceeds) seems to be when he sent her the following anguished telegram at her mother's address:

MY DARLING I JUST WANTED TO LET YOU KNOW REGARDLESS OF THE THINGS WE HAVE TO EXPERIENCE IN LIFE I WANT YOU TO KNOW THAT I AM IN THE GROUND NOW I WOULD SHOOT MYSELF FOR YOU IF I HAD A GUN BUT I DONT HAVE ONE TELL MY WIFE THE MOST HORRIBLE THING IN THE WORLD IS SILENCE AND AM EXPERIENCING SAME. IM TIRED AND GOING TO SLEEP   CHARLES PARKER

After finishing two final weeks at Birdland, he was dependent on friends such as Dave Lambert (who led the singers on the Gil Evans date) to arrange appearances such as those at the Sunday night sessions at a Greenwich Village coffee house called the Open Door, produced by Robert Reisner. Already, the historic concert at Toronto's Massey Hall had been organised, not through the agency, but at the initiative of a group of Canadian fans.

As recorded by Charles Mingus and Max Roach and issued on their Debut label, the Massey Hall performance was the only one of the numerous 'live' releases of which Charlie was aware (apart from the Jazz At The Phil concerts) and it required the use of the pseudonym 'Charlie Chan' to get around his exclusive recording contract with Granz. No one made much money from the record, at least before its 1970s reissue, as the Debut label soon went out of business, but Charlie was the only one to get full payment for the actual concert – seeing the unexpectedly small attendance, he had demanded the box-office cash instead of the bouncing cheques accepted by the others. The historical significance was simply that of the last-ever quintet performance of Parker, Gillespie, Powell and Roach together and, though none of the material was written later than 1944, the musicians' exciting rediscovery of each other makes it sound absolutely fresh. Though much has been made of supposed rivalry between Charlie and Dizzy, Charlie's solo work is notably relaxed throughout and especially on *Perdido* and *Hot House*. It is worth noting, however, that while Dizzy had just come through a difficult period artistically, and was about to become a valuable property in Granz's touring stable, Charlie had not been part of Jazz At The Phil since 1950 and his career – unlike his playing – had completely lost its impetus.

Charlie's studio tracks from the same period do not even hint at this, though, perhaps because with one exception they all have Max Roach on drums. The Miles Davis session would have also broken his record contract (and he received an advance payment to do so, rather than just turning up unexpectedly) except that it was not issued till after his death, due to a shortage of material not unconnected with the fact that Charlie fell asleep during the recording. This second and last time he was to be heard playing tenor saxophone on record is naturally of interest and, if his tone is somewhat unfocussed, this is doubtless because he needed a much harder reed than the borrowed instrument provided. As for Charlie's own quartet dates (in December 1952 and August 1953) they are filled with buoyant solos on previously composed themes such as *Confirmation, Chi Chi* and another 'Swedish blues' dedicated to *Laird Baird*, and on the themeless improvisations *Cosmic Rays* and *Kim*.

Family life was, as we have seen, far from buoyant and Charlie's letter of February 1953 to the State Liquor Authority underlines the reason (though why he should write *after* working the New York clubs again since the previous September is not clear, unless he was on some kind of six-month trial period):

> My right to pursue my chosen profession has been taken away, and my wife and three children who are innocent of any wrongdoing are suffering . . . My baby girl [Pree] is a city case in the hospital because her health has been neglected since we hadn't the necessary doctor fees.

The financial and emotional strain was beginning to tell on Chan, for later the same year she wrote an extremely troubled letter to Charlie, saying among other things:

> I know how unsettled you are as far as every day living is concerned. How unable to forgive the hurts of the world . . . And, although I want with all my heart to believe in your moral reform, I know that there would be backslides . . . But I'm afraid. Somewhere during our three years I lost my courage.

Chan cannot have been too pleased when, probably at her

suggestion, the Moe Gale agency took over Charlie's bookings and, on one of his first dates for them, he managed to get reported to the musicians' union after the first day of a week in Montreal and then summarily fired on the third day. Despite Charlie's counterclaim the union's financial adjudication was in favour of the Montreal club.

Several appearances in Chicago and Boston, at least one in concert with the strings, and an 11-day tour of the West Coast with an all-star package, kept Charlie reasonably busy into the New Year. And, while in Boston again in January, he heard that he was to join in mid-tour the 'Festival of Modern Jazz' package with Stan Kenton, Erroll Garner, Dizzy Gillespie and others – the nationwide concert package had just been deprived of Stan Getz following his arrest for drug offences (but, because of Charlie's own reputation, it took a Charlie Parker *and* a Lee Konitz to replace one Getz). As the tour ended on the West Coast, Norman Granz arranged a recording session which might have been one of the greatest in jazz history or might have been a disappointment; Charlie was present and correct but his co-star Art Tatum was indisposed and, in the light of subsequent events, there was no time to reschedule the date.

Immediately after the last concert of the tour on February 28, Charlie was booked again for a week at the Tiffany, but he was soon in trouble with the club management for disappearing on the first night. Charlie's explanation was simple: he had been 'taken to a Los Angeles Police Station on suspicion of being a user of narcotics. I was held there over night, and after it was found out that the charges could not be substantiated, as a substitute, I was booked on a drunken and disorderly charge which was unfounded.' The suspicion was, however, correct despite the lack of evidence, and he was drinking very heavily. He had indeed been fired yet again by this time he received word that two-year-old Pree had died in hospital. Charlie's telegrams to Chan betray the sobering impact of this tragic news:

[*Time of dispatch*] 4.11 AM
MY DARLING MY DAUGHTER'S DEATH SURPRISED ME MORE THAN IT DID YOU DON'T FULFILL FUNERAL PROCEEDINGS UNTIL I GET THERE I SHALL BE THE FIRST ONE TO WALK

INTO OUR CHAPEL FORGIVE ME FOR NOT BEING THERE WITH
YOU WHILE YOU WERE AT THE HOSPITAL
YOURS MOST SINCERELY YOUR HUSBAND CHARLIE PARKER

4.13 AM
MY DARLING FOR GOD'S SAKE HOLD ON TO YOURSELF
CHAS PARKER

4.15 AM
CHAN, HELP
CHARLIE PARKER

As if this weren't enough, there were still financial worries. Chan
has said that he accepted the tour with Stan Kenton 'Because so
much loot was involved', but after paying $500.00 owed to Billy
Shaw and a sum not much smaller for funeral expenses, he was
once again in debt to his new agency. Then, in the matter of the
Tiffany Club's complaint, the union's award went against
Charlie. There was still recording as a source of immediate
income but, on the only two sessions he made in 1954, little was
produced and nothing that was not rather ordinary by Charlie's
own standards. He was still obliged to take gigs in Philadelphia,
Baltimore, Chicago and Detroit to defray his fine. One pleasant
interlude in late July and August was at the Red Barn on Cape
Cod, where Chan joined him to attempt to repair their
relationship. But the self-destruction began again at the end of
August on an engagement with the strings at Birdland, Charlie's
first appearance there in over a year. As if to demonstrate the
inflexibility of working with non-jazz musicians, he asked for *East
of the Sun* but followed the strings' introduction by playing
Dancing in the Dark: and then, as if to prove that he didn't
desperately need this gig, he publicly fired the band for their
incompetence. Not unnaturally, Birdland then fired Bird.

Realising that the union was now quite likely to order him to
pay the musicians' salaries for the rest of the scheduled three
weeks, he next tried to commit suicide by swallowing iodine and
was committed to Bellevue, the New York mental hospital. (Later
he claimed that he had faked the suicide in order to evade his
responsibilities, but this seems to amount to the same thing.)
Despite evidence of genuine emotional problems he was soon
discharged in the care of Chan and the family doctor. And,

despite having been cancelled from a European tour due for late September, he was added instead to a concert bill in both New York and Boston with Count Basie, Sarah Vaughan and the Modern Jazz Quartet. Two days later, in other words less than three weeks after leaving Bellevue, he was back again at his own request, seeking an escape from both chronic alcoholism and the broken promises to Chan. Two-and-a-half weeks later, he was discharged again and went with Chan and the children to stay with her mother in Pennsylvania. Two weeks later, by the time of Robert Reisner's concert at New York Town Hall, he appeared to be getting used to spending all his free time in the country and travelling to the city to visit the agency and the psychiatrist at the hospital.

But it was not to last. As soon as he started doing regular gigs again, he started missing the train back to the country and began living on the charity of friends and chance acquaintances. A week after the Town Hall concert Hot Lips Page, once the trumpet king of Kansas City, died aged only 46 and Charlie, who paid his respects at the funeral parlour, was already wondering out loud whether he would see 1955. Later, he took to visiting the city morgue to survey unidentified corpses, claiming that he was looking for a friend of his. In Chicago in January, he was advised to wear an overcoat but declined with the words, 'I don't want to see another winter – pneumonia's next for me.' It was during this same weekend that, after spending most of the evening delaying his performance and simultaneously getting in a state where he was unable to perform, he had to endure an effusive hipster who told him how well he had played and what a great guy he was generally. He finally rounded on his sycophantic tormentor and yelled, 'Look, man, I *goofed*. And I know it!'

There was a final engagement at Birdland for two days at the start of March. Not so much a comeback, more a come-back-all-is-forgiven-just-this-once. A special all-star quintet was assembled with Art Blakey, Charles Mingus, Kenny Dorham and Bud Powell, and on the first night the performance was, at the least, perfectly adequate. But on March 5 the pianist, who was frequently more disturbed than Charlie was, also got drunk quicker; there were verbal altercations and not much music. Finally, as Powell was being helped from the bandstand, the leader announced his name, repeatedly, ironically, contemptuously. No one applauded, ever again.

The following week, before setting out for a gig in Boston, Charlie felt unwell and called at the apartment of the Baroness Nica de Koenigswarter, sister of Lord Rothschild but also a friend to Art Blakey, Thelonious Monk and others in the jazz community. She had Charlie attended by her doctor, who insisted on him remaining where he was since he refused to enter hospital, and for three days Nica and her daughter took care of him. On the last day of his life, March 12, Charlie let Nica play a few of his records for the doctor, giving pride of place to *Just Friends* and *April in Paris*, with strings. And the heart attack which ended his suffering came while watching the Dorsey Brothers on television, in order to admire once again the technical efficiency and emotional vacuity of altoist Jimmy Dorsey.

Apparently Charlie had been granted his wish and had contracted pneumonia. But, as well as his long-standing ulcers, he now had advanced cirrhosis. The narcotics had left fewer marks, especially during the year since the death of Pree, but as Charlie once said, 'They can get it out of your blood, but they can't get it out of your mind.' From the condition of his 34-year-old body, the doctor estimated Charlie's age at the time of death to be 53.

Chapter Eight

The rootless confusion of Charlie Parker's private life and the waste of his undoubted intellect can perhaps be written off by some as the fault of society (though no less of a tragedy for him, of course). But, whether it is seen as imposed on him or totally self-inflicted, his downfall ultimately pales into insignificance before his musical legacy.

This legacy has two distinct aspects. As it happens, the time would be ripe for a detailed study of the altoist's profound effect on other instrumentalists and composers, although in some cases this would be difficult to separate from the influence of the bebop movement as a whole. But the nearest we can come to this, within the scope of the present book, is to study Parker's own style through the tangible evidence of his live and studio recordings. They afford not only a joyful voyage of discovery but a considerable challenge to anyone wanting to penetrate beneath the brilliant surface and the direct emotionalism. And even these aspects present their problems, since they have often proved too strong meat for listeners coming from different backgrounds. Among Parker devotees, his instrumental tone means diverse things to diverse people, and the most profound musical comment in Ross Russell's book is relevant here:

> The sound has its double edge, the two tones combined in one, the thin transparent tone and the fat thick tone, one on top of the other, blended into a single textured sound. It is at once veiled and clear, cloudy and incandescent.

Like that of all the major jazz soloists, Parker's personal sound is emotionally ambiguous, and indeed this is the nature of his relationship to the music of the blues. He rarely employed blues phraseology, and when he did it formed a deliberate contrast to his normal melodic style, but it is his tone which on an emotional level turned everything he played into a blues, no matter how involved its contours.

With a view to meeting the challenge of the contours, a bit of detail may be of help 'to less technically minded readers. (Actually, in my experience, the non-players are often more aware of the limitations of musical description and analysis, and therefore gain more from it, than musicians or would-be musicians. Those without an instrument at their fingertips can find a creative awareness of the Parker style by memorising particular passages and either whistling along with the records or singing them in the bath.) It is the rhythmic variety of his playing which is now so totally accepted – in theory, at any rate – that it becomes hard to appreciate until one attempts an actual imitation. Even Dizzy Gillespie, a performer of great rhythmic intensity but before the mid-1940s a trifle stiff, has said, 'Rhythmically, he was quite advanced, with setting up the phrase and how you got from one note to another . . . After we started playing together, I began to play, rhythmically, more like him. In that sense he influenced me, and all of us, because what makes the style is not what you play but how you play it.' Interestingly, this is the aspect which shows the clearest derivation from Lester Young, but the art of creating an improvisation with an apparent rhythmic life of its own (derived ultimately from Armstrong) was, in Lester's case, deployed in a constant ebb and flow of tensions between on-the-beat playing and around-the-beat playing. Parker's comparatively 'hard' approach produced a consistent level of rhythmic tautness by playing continually just behind the beat, and maintaining the same relationship to the stated pulse of a rhythm-section despite all the cross-accents he introduced.

The accentuation of every third beat or every third half-beat during two or more bars (of 4-to-the-bar meter) is fundamental to all Afro-American music, and goes back at least as far as the opening bars of both *Maple Leaf Rag* and *The Entertainer*. In Parker's compositions it appears, for instance, in *Billie's Bounce* (bars 1-4, 11-12), *Another Hair-Do* (bars 1-3) and *Moose the Mooche* (bars 1-4, 15-16, 31-32). (It is particularly useful to be able to draw examples from his written melodies because, except from the occasional simple riff tune such as *Cool Blues* and *Buzzy*, they relate directly to his improvisational style and, as we have seen, some of them were created almost as fast.) During improvisation, this became such a central principle – constant yet constantly varied as to the starting note – that the effect is overlooked in its total integration with the harmonic and melodic shapes. This is, of course, what makes Parker's music so comparable to the work of a present-day Latin-American rhythmic-section, whereas unfortunately the Machito band of Parker's day, though 'modern' for its time (prior to the influence of bebop itself on Latin music), stuck to specific dance beats with a minimum of rhythmic improvisation. hearing the classic Parker quintet play the themes of *Barbados*, *Bongo Beep* or the remarkable *Bongo Bop* (with its 1st, 5th and 9th bars 'Latin' and the remainder 'straight'), one realizes that Max Roach was actually the most compatible Latin drummer to play with Parker. But it is also obvious that these particular themes could well be played with a straight rhythm-section, whereas all the others such as *Billie's Bounce* or *Moose the Mooche* could be played Latin, without altering the melody line or its accentuation. If further proof is required of the prime importance of rhythm in Parker's music, it may be found in Sadik Hakim's comment that, when demonstrating a new tune, 'He had a funny way of humming the rhythm of the tune instead of the melody.'

Harmonically speaking, there is much potential confusion in the statements of other musicians. Drummer Gus Johnson has said of the Jay McShann period, 'We would play a number in five or six different keys – what we call chromatics. We'd start in B-flat and then take just a half-step [i.e. to B], to C, to C-sharp . . . Charlie would just run all through 'm.' This sort of thing, presumably for a chorus at a time, was put on record later by Stan Getz (*Crazy Chords*) and goes to show the preliminary work which went into another aspect of the same period, described by Gene Ramey: 'Bird had a way of starting on *a B natural against the B flat chord* and he would run a cycle against that' (my italics, as this remark has usually been misquoted). The reference this time is to a rapid series of substitutions, better outlined in one of his rare interviews by Don Byas: 'Bird got a lot of things from me . . . I played all that stuff from Tatum. That F-sharp, B-natural, E, A, D, G, C, F, like in [*I got*] *Rhythm*, instead of playing *Rhythm* chords.' Most revealingly, however, it is hard to find recorded examples of anything so straightforward or elementyary in Parker's playing. Tatum seems not to have put this on record until his 1944 *I Got Rhythm* although Monk, who doubtless also fot it from Tatum, can be heard doing it on *Rhythm Riff*, a 1941 live recording at Minton's, as well as on later items such as *Humph* and *Rhythm-a-ning*. But, out of all Parker's output, apart from a brief reference in *Merry-Go-Round* and during the recording from the 1950 Swedish tour, this approach only survives in the chord-sequence of *Confirmation* and the related idea of the 'Swedish blues' such as *Blues for Alice* and *Laird Baird*.

As far as improvisation is concerned, these particular substitutions must have been solely a phenomenon of his apprentice period. What distinguished his mature style was the ability to take *any* principle of chord complication, whether derived from Tatum, Ellington, Gillespie or Lester Young, and make it work in a totally non-programmed and non-schematic way. Kenny Clarke has said, 'Bird was twice as fast as Prez

[Young] and into harmony Prez hadn't touched', and naturally this impression was aided by the rhythmic freedom previously described; for instance, the chromatic passing-chord in bar 3 of Parker's solo in *Shaw 'Nuff* begins on the fourth beat, i.e. later than expected, but in bar 11 reappears early as the second beat. In fact, what appear to be substitute chords are often merely anticipated or delayed chords, as in the first 8 bars of the 1951 Birdland solo on *Anthropology* which include both an anticipation (end of bar 3) and a delay (end of bar 7). As to the actual 'new' harmony Parker incorporated, Dexter Gordon is fairly specific: '[Young] was playing the 6th and the 9th . . . Then Bird extended that to 11ths and 13ths, like Diz, and to altered notes like the flatted 5th the the flatted 9th.' Already common in Tatum's chording these, of course, are the 'higher intervals' referred to in Parker's own statement about his discoveries, which is nevertheless more than somewhat misleading since it implies that he then started using them extensively. Except again perhaps during his apprenticeship, this is not the case except in the sense that temporary reference to an alien key-signature (i.e. polytonality, or what became known in the post-Coltrane era as 'side-slipping') could be construed as a use of the higher intervals of the original key. Later in the same *Anthropology* solo just mentioned, bars 9-10 of the third chorus are an example of a phrase repeated a semitone higher, thus clashing with the original chords, but this – like Parker's highly chromatic middle-8s on *Red Cross* and *Shaw 'Nuff* – is something he used extremely sparingly after 1945.

In a purely melodic sense, repetition of an improvised phrase at a different pitch is a device probably derived from Parker's high-school acquaintance with European music. The first two bars of *Embraceable You*, the opening phrase of the *Just Friends* solo, and the quotation from *Cocktails for Two* near the end of *Warming Up a Riff* are perhaps the best-known examples, but much subtler uses of repetition or of imitation (i.e. approximate repetition) are to be found in many improvisations. They also point our attention towards the classical sense of melodic and rhythmic balance that informs those beautiful written melodies such as *Confirmation* and *Quasimado*, both of which have recently had words added by singer Sheila Jordan. The former has been described as a continuous, non-repeating melody, but in fact the first 8, the second 8 and the last 8 are extremely closely related, and it is instructive how one small difference necessitates another small difference which necessitates yet another small difference, in order to retain a perfect overall balance. Exactly the same process is used in improvisation, where Parker's melodic sense reveals his absorption of all the best 18th and 19th-century European composers, which is doubtless the reason for his subsequent feeling that he was repeating himself and for his interest in 20th-century Europeans. Allied to his great harmonic expertise, it is also the reason why the next generation of jazzmen felt that the European aspects of jazz could never be more fully exploited than by Parker, and that it was time for something else.

But what he perhaps did not have the confidence to realize was that his particular combination of European and African elements was a more complex than any previously achieved, and that it was capable of infinite variation. The rhythmic subtlety which is crucial to *Confirmation* and *Quasimado* also give life to, and is enlivened by, the melodic ambiguity of a theme like *Bird Feathers*, which in terms pf pitch opens out almost a pair of wings and then hovers around an unstated central note. Such a theme also remind us that, as well as the rhythmic variety within a phrase and the modification of the rate of harmonic changes, Parker also uses a melodic 'macro-syncopation' of the length of phrases (a lack of which easily identifies tunes attributed to but not written by Parker, such as *Ornithology* and Miles Davis' *Donna Lee*). Similarly during improvisations, which required control of the minutest rhythmic and harmonic details, Parker was able to mould huge blocks of sound or unequal weight and still impart a precise balance to the whole. In this way his style would have been capable not only of infinite variation but of infinite extension; the statements of such varied witnesses as Barry Ulanov and Sam Rivers that towards the end of his career he was playing longer and longer solos should cause regret that the 1951 Boston recording is virtually the only one extant from a completely unfettered jam-session situation.

For those interested in pursuing the technicalities a little further, there is first of all, if you have access to it, the excellent essay by James Patrick accompanying the 5-LP Savoy album.

David Baker's *Charlie Parker: Alto Saxophone* (Shattings/Hansen) has the advantages of longer musical examples and, while most of the volumes of music alone need to be approached with some caution, a veritable cornucopia of accurate transcriptions is contained in the *Charlie Parker Omnibook* (Atlantic Music Corporation).

DISCOGRAPHY

In the chronological listing I have attempted to include everything so far released featuring Charlie Parker, with what I believe to be its first issue number. These are cross-referenced to recent issues at the end of the discography, and in both of these lists I have been assisted not only by previous publications but also by Ed Dipple, Graham Griffiths, Tony Middleton, Chris Sheridan and Ray Smith.

The instrumental abbreviations are as follows:– (arr) arranger, (as) alto saxophone, (b) bass, (bgo) bongo, (bs) baritone saxophone, (bsn) bassoon, (cel) cello, (cga) conga, (cl) clarinet, (cond) conductor, (d) drums, (eng-h) english horn, (f) flute, (fr-h) french horn, (g) guitar, (mca) maraccas, (ob) oboe, (org) organ, (p) piano, (perc) percussion, (ss) soprano saxophone, (tb) trombone, (tbl) timbales, (tp) trumpet, (ts) tenor saxophone, (v) and (vcl) vocal, (vib) vibraphone, (vla) viola, (vln) violin, (vtb) valve-trombone, *incomplete, **edited recording.

BRIAN PRIESTLEY, London, February 1984

JAY McSHANN AND HIS ORCHESTRA
Buddy Anderson, Orville Minor (tp), Bob Gould (tb, vln), Charlie Parker (as), William J. Scott (ts), Jay McShann (p), Gene Ramey (b), Gus Johnson (d). *Station KFBI, Wichita, November 30, 1940*

	I FOUND A NEW BABY	(1) Onyx ORI221
	BODY AND SOUL	(1) Onyx ORI221

Bob Mabane (ts) replaces Scott   *Station KFBI, Wichita, December 2, 1940*

	HONEYSUCKLE ROSE	(1) Onyx ORI221
	LADY BE GOOD	(1) Onyx ORI221
	COQUETTE	(1) Onyx ORI221
	MOTEN SWING	(1) Onyx ORI221
	BLUES	(1) Onyx ORI221

Buddy Anderson, Orville Minor, Harold Bruce (tp), Taswell Baird (tb), Charlie Parker, John Jackson (as), Bob Mabane, Harold Ferguson (ts), Jay McShann (p), Gene Ramey (b), Gus Johnson (d), Walter Brown (vcl). *Dallas, April 30, 1941*

93730A	SWINGMATISM	(2) Decca 8570
93731A	HOOTIE BLUES vWB	(2) Decca 8559
93732A	DEXTER BLUES	(2) Decca 8583

Bob Merrill (tp), Fred Culliver (ts) replace Bruce and Ferguson, Lawrence Anderson (tb), James Coe (bs), Lucky Enois (g), Al Hibbler (vcl) added. *NYC, July 2, 1942*

70993A	LONELY BOY BLUES vWB	(2) Decca 4387
70994A	GET ME ON YOUR MIND vAH	(2) Decca 4418
70995A	THE JUMPIN' BLUES vWB	(2) Decca 4418
70996A	SEPIAN BOUNCE	(2) Decca 4387

CHARLIE PARKER
Charlie Parker (as) with unknown musicians poss. incl. George Treadwell, Vic Coulsen (tp). *Poss. Monroe's Uptown House, NYC, c. 1942*

	CHEROKEE	(1) Onyx ORI221

69

TINY GRIMES QUINTET
Charlie Parker (as), Clyde Hart (p), Tiny Grimes (g, vcl), Jimmy Butts (b), Doc West (d). *NYC, September 15, 1944*

S5710-1	TINY'S TEMPO	(3,4) Savoy MG12001*
S5710-2	TINY'S TEMPO	(3,5) Savoy MG12001*
S5710-3	TINY'S TEMPO	(3,6) Savoy 526
S5711-1	I'LL ALWAYS LOVE YOU vTG	(3,7) Savoy SJL2208
S5711-2	I'LL ALWAYS LOVE YOU vTG	(3,6) Savoy 526
S5712-1	ROMANCE WITHOUT FINANCE vTG	(3,7) Savoy SJL2208
S5712-2	ROMANCE WITHOUT FINANCE vTG	(3) Savoy S5J5500*
S5712-3	ROMANCE WITHOUT FINANCE vTG	(3,5) Savoy SJL1107
S5712-4	ROMANCE WITHOUT FINANCE vTG	(3) Savoy S5J5500*
S5712-5	ROMANCE WITHOUT FINANCE vTG	(3,6) Savoy 532
S5713-1	RED CROSS	(3,5) Savoy MG12001*
S5713-2	RED CROSS	(3,6) Savoy 532

CLYDE HART ALL STARS
Dizzy Gillespie (tp), Trummy Young (tb, vcl), Charlie Parker (as), Don Byas (ts), Clyde Hart (p), Mike Bryan (g), Al Hall (b), Specs Powell (d), Rubberlegs Williams (vcl). *NYC, January 1945*

W3301	WHAT'S THE MATTER NOW? vRW	(8) Continental 6013
W3302	I WANT EVERY BIT OF IT vRW	(8) Continental 6020
W3303	THAT'S THE BLUES vRW	(8) Continental 6013
W3304	4-F BLUES vRW	(8) Continental 6020
W3304 (alt.)	G.I. BLUES vRW	(8) Plymouth P100-38
W3305	DREAM OF YOU vTY	(8) Continental 6060
W3306	SEVENTH AVENUE vTY	(8) Continental 6005
W3307	SORTA KINDA vTY	(8) Continental 6005
W3308	OH, OH, MY, MY vTY	(8) Continental 6060

COOTIE WILLIAMS AND HIS ORCHESTRA
Money Johnson, Ermit Perry, George Treadwell, Cootie Williams (tp), Ed Burke, Bob Horton (tb), Frank Powell, Charlie Parker (as), Lee Pope, Sam Taylor (ts), Ed deVerteuil (bs), Arnold Jarvis (p), Leroy Kirkland (g), Carl Pruitt (b), Vess Payne (d), Toni Warren (vcl). *Savoy Ballroom, NYC, February 12, 1945*

'ROUND MIDNIGHT (theme)	(8) One Night Stand 582
711	(8) One Night Stand 582
DO NOTHIN' TILL YOU HEAR	(8) One Night Stand 582
DON'T BLAME ME	(8) One Night Stand 582
PERDIDO	(8) One Night Stand 582
NIGHT CAP	(8) One Night Stand 582
SATURDAY NIGHT vTW	(8) One Night Stand 582
FLOOGIE BOO - 1	(8) One Night Stand 582
ST. LOUIS BLUES	(8) One Night Stand 582*

1-Williams, Parker, Taylor, Jarvis, Pruitt and Payne only.

DIZZY GILLESPIE SEXTET
Dizzy Gillespie (tp), Charlie Parker (as), Clyde Hart (p), Remo Palmier (g), Slam Stewart (b), Cozy Cole (d). *NYC, February 1945*

G554-1	GROOVIN' HIGH	(9) Guild 1001
G556	ALL THE THINGS YOU ARE	(9) Musicraft 488
G557	DIZZY ATMOSPHERE	(9) Musicraft 488

DIZZY GILLESPIE AND HIS ALL STAR QUINTET

Dizzy Gillespie (tp, vcl), Charlie Parker (as), Al Haig (p), Curley Russell (b), Sid Catlett (d), Sarah Vaughan (vcl). *NYC, May 11, 1945*

G565–A1	SALT PEANUTS vDG	(9) Guild 1003
G566A–1	SHAW NUFF	(9) Guild 1002
G567A–1	LOVER MAN vSV	(9) Guild 1002
G568A–1	HOT HOUSE	(9) Guild 1003

SARAH VAUGHAN

Dizzy Gillespie (tp), Charlie Parker (as), Flip Phillips (ts), Nat Jaffe-1, Tadd Dameron-2 (p), Bill DeArango (g), Curley Russell (b), Max Roach (d), Sarah Vaughan (vcl). *NYC, May 25, 1945*

W3325	WHAT MORE CAN A WOMAN DO? -1	(8) Continental 6008
W3326	I'D RATHER HAVE A MEMORY THAN A DREAM -2	(8) Continental 6008
W3327	MEAN TO ME -1	(8) Continental 6024

RED NORVO AND HIS SELECTED SEXTET

Dizzy Gillespie (tp), Charlie Parker (as), Flip Phillips (ts), Teddy Wilson (p), Red Norvo (vib), Slam Stewart (b), Specs Powell -1, J. C. Heard -2 (d). *NYC, June 6, 1945*

T8–A	HALLELUJAH -1	(10) Dial LP903
T8–B	HALLELUJAH -1	(10) Dial 1045
T8–F	HALLELUJAH -1	(10) Comet T6
T9–B	GET HAPPY -1	(10) Dial 1035
T9–D	GET HAPPY -1	(10) Comet T7
T10–A	SLAM SLAM BLUES (BIRD BLUES) -2	(10) Dial 1045
T10–B	SLAM SLAM BLUES -2	(10) Comet T6
T11–AA	CONGO BLUES -2	(10) Dial LP903*
T11–BB	CONGO BLUES -2	(10) Dial LP903*
T11–A	CONGO BLUES -2	(10) Dial LP903*
T11–B	CONGO BLUES -2	(10) Dial 1035
T11–C	CONGO BLUES -2	(10) Comet T7

SIR CHARLES AND HIS ALL STARS

Buck Clayton (tp), Charlie Parker (as), Dexter Gordon (ts), Sir Charles Thompson (p), Danny Barker (g), Jimmy Butts (b), J. C. Heard (d). *NYC, September 4, 1945*

R1030	TAKIN' OFF	(8) Apollo 757
R1031	IF I HAD YOU	(8) Apollo 757
R1032	20TH CENTURY BLUES	(8) Apollo 759
R1033	THE STREET BEAT	(8) Apollo 759

CHARLIE PARKER'S REE BOPPERS

Miles Davis (tp -1), Dizzy Gillespie (tp -2, p -3), Charlie Parker (as), Sadik Hakim (p -4), Curley Russell (b), Max Roach (d). *NYC, November 26, 1945*

S5850–1	BILLIE'S BOUNCE -1,3	(3,4) Savoy MG12079
S5850–2	BILLIE'S BOUNCE -1,3	(3) Savoy MG12079*
S5850–3	BILLIE'S BOUNCE -1,3	(3,5) Savoy MG12079
S5849	WARMING UP A RIFF -3	(3,6) Savoy 945*
S5850–4	BILLIE'S BOUNCE -1,3	(3) Savoy MG12079*
S5851–5	BILLIE'S BOUNCE -1,3	(3,6) Savoy 573
S5851–1	NOW'S THE TIME -1, 3	(3) Savoy MG12079*

S5851–2	NOW'S THE TIME -1,3	(3) Savoy MG12079*
S5851–3	NOW'S THE TIME -1,3	(3,5) Savoy MG12079
S5851–4	NOW'S THE TIME -1,3	(3,6) Savoy 573
S5852–1	THRIVING FROM A RIFF -1,4	(3,5) Savoy MG12079
S5852–2	THRIVING FROM A RIFF -1,4	(3) Savoy MG12079*
S5852–3	THRIVING FROM A RIFF -1,4	(3,6) Savoy 903
	MEANDERING -3	(3,6) Savoy MG12079*
S5853–1	KO-KO -2,4	(3) Savoy MG12079*
S5853–2	KO-KO (CO-COA) -2,3	(3,6) Savoy 597

SLIM GAILLARD
Dizzy Gillespie (tp), Charlie Parker (as), Jack McVea (ts), Dodo Marmarosa (p), Slim Gaillard (g, p-1, vcl), Bam Brown (b, vcl), Zutty Singleton (d). *LA, December 1945*

BTJ38–?	DIZZY BOOGIE -1	(8) Polydor 545.107
BTJ38–2	DIZZY BOOGIE -1	(8,11) Bel-Tone 753
BTJ39–?	FLAT FOOT FLOOGIE	(8,11) Halo 50273
BTJ39–2	FLAT FOOT FLOOGIE	(8) Bel-Tone 758
BTJ40–2	POPPITY POP	(8,11) Bel-Tone 753
BTJ41–RE	SLIM'S JAM	(8,11) Bel-Tone 761

DIZZY GILLESPIE AND HIS REBOP SIX
Dizzy Gillespie (tp), Charlie Parker (as), Al Haig (p), Milt Jackson (vib -1), Ray Brown (b), Stan Levey (d). *LA, December 1945*

JUB161	GROOVIN' HIGH	(12) Main-Man BFWHCB617
JUB162	SHAW NUFF	(12) Spotlite SPJ123
JUB163	DIZZY ATMOSPHERE -1	(12) Klacto MG102
Lucky Thompson (ts) added		*LA, January 1946*
	SALT PEANUTS -1 vDG	(12) Meexa Discox 1776

JAZZ AT THE PHILHARMONIC
Dizzy Gillespie, Al Killian (tp), Charlie Parker, Willie Smith (as), Lester Young, Charlie Ventura (ts), Mel Powell (p), Billy Hadnott (d), Lee Young (d). *LA, January 1946*

413/414	SWEET GEORGIA BROWN	(13) Disc 2004

Howard McGhee (tp), Arnold Ross (p) replace Gillespie and Powell, Ventura out.

D241/2	BLUES FOR NORMAN	(13) Disc 2001
D243/4	I CAN'T GET STARTED	(13) Disc 2002
D245/6	LADY BE GOOD	(13) Disc 2005
D247/8	AFTER YOU'VE GONE	(13) Disc 5100

DIZZY GILLESPIE JAZZMEN
Dizzy Gillespie (tp), Charlie Parker (as), Lucky Thompson (ts), George Handy (p), Arv Garrison (g), Ray Brown (b), Stan Levey (d). *LA, February 7, 1946*

D1000	DIGGIN' DIZ (BONGO BEEP)	(14) Dial 1004

CHARLIE PARKER QUINTET
Miles Davis (tp), Charlie Parker (as), Joe Albany (p), Addison Farmer (b), Chuck Thompson (d). *Finale Club, LA, March 1946*

	ANTHROPOLOGY	(12) Queen-Disc Q–017
	BILLIE'S BOUNCE	(12) Queen-Disc Q–017
	BLUE 'N' BOOGIE	(12) Queen-Disc Q–017

| | ALL THE THINGS YOU ARE | (12) Queen-Disc Q–017 |
| | ORNITHOLOGY | (12) Queen-Disc Q–017* |

CHARLIE PARKER SEPTET

Miles Davis (tp), Charlie Parker (as), Lucky Thompson (ts), Dodo Marmarosa (p), Arv Garrison (g -1), Vic McMillan (b), Roy Porter (d). *LA, March 28, 1946*

D1010–1	MOOSE THE MOOCHE	(14) Dial DLP201
D1010–2	MOOSE THE MOOCHE	(14) Dial 1003, 1004
D1010–3	MOOSE THE MOOCHE	(14) Spotlite 105, 101
D1011–1	YARDBIRD SUITE -1	(14) Dial DLP201
D1011–4	YARDBIRD SUITE -1	(14) Dial 1003
D1012–1	ORNITHOLOGY -1	(14) Dial DLP208
D1012–3	BIRD LORE (ORNITHOLOGY) -1	(14) Dial 1006
D1012–4	ORNITHOLOGY -1	(14) Dial 1002
D1013–1	FAMOUS ALTO BREAK -1	(14) Dial DLP905*
D1013–4	NIGHT IN TUNISIA -1	(14) Dial DLP201
D1013–5	NIGHT IN TUNISIA -1	(14) Dial 1002

WILLIE SMITH/BENNY CARTER/CHARLIE PARKER

Willie Smith -1, Benny Carter -2, Charlie Parker -3, (as), Nat King Cole (p), Oscar Moore (g), Johnny Miller (b), Buddy Rich (d). *LA, March/April 1946*

| | MEDLEY: TEA FOR TWO -1/BODY AND SOUL -2/CHEROKEE -3 | (12) Spotlite SPJ123 |
| | ORNITHOLOGY -3 | (12) Spotlite SPJ123* |

JAZZ AT THE PHILHARMONIC

Buck Clayton (tp), Willie Smith, Charlie Parker (as), Lester Young, Coleman Hawkins (ts), Kenny Kersey (p), Irving Ashby (g), Billy Hadnott (b), Buddy Rich (d). *Embassy Theatre, LA, April 22, 1946*

| 101/2/3/4 | JATP BLUES | (13) Clef 101/102 |
| | I GOT RHYTHM | (13) Mercury MG35014 |

CHARLIE PARKER QUINTET/HOWARD McGHEE QUINTET

Howard McGhee (tp), Charlie Parker (as), Jimmy Bunn (p), Bob Kesterton (b), Roy Porter (d). *LA, July 29, 1946*

D1021–A	MAX IS MAKING WAX	(14) Jazztone J1004
D1022–A	LOVER MAN	(14) Dial 1007
D1023–A	THE GYPSY	(14) Dial 1043
D1024–A	BEBOP	(14) Dial 1007

CHARLIE PARKER

Charlie Parker (as), Russ Freeman (p), Arnold Fishkind (b), Jimmy Pratt (d). *LA, February 1, 1947*

D901/2	LULLABY IN RHYTHM	(15) Spotlite 107*
K903	HOME COOKING III	(16) Dial LP905*
K904	HOME COOKING II	(16) Dial LP905*
K905	HOME COOKING I	(16) Dial LP905*
	YARDBIRD SUITE -1	(15) Spotlite 107*

1- Howard McGhee, Shorty Rogers, Melvyn Broiles (tp) added.

CHARLIE PARKER QUARTET

Charlie Parker (as), Erroll Garner (p), Red Callender (b), Doc West (d), Earl Coleman (vcl). *LA, February 19, 1947*

D1051-C	THIS IS ALWAYS vEC	(17) Dial 1015, 1019
D1051-D	THIS IS ALWAYS vEC	(17) Dial LP202
D1052-A	DARK SHADOWS vEC	(17) Dial LP202
D1052-B	DARK SHADOWS vEC	(17) Dial LP901
D1052-C	DARK SHADOWS vEC	(17) Dial 1014
D1052-D	DARK SHADOWS vEC	(17) Spotlite 105, 102
D1053-A	BIRD'S NEST	(17) Dial 1014
D1053-B	BIRD'S NEST	(17) Dial LP905
D1053-C	BIRD'S NEST	(17) Dial 1014
D1054-A	HOT BLUES (BLOWTOP BLUES)	(17) Dial LP202
D1054-B	BLOWTOP BLUES (COOL BLUES)	(17) Dial LP901
D1054-C	COOL BLUES	(17) Dial 1015
D1054-D	COOL BLUES	(17) Dial LP901

CHARLIE PARKER'S NEW STARS

Howard McGhee (tp), Charlie Parker (as), Wardell Gray (ts), Dodo Marmarosa (p), Barney Kessel (g), Red Callender (b), Don Lamond (d). *LA, February 26, 1947*

D1071-A	RELAXIN' AT CAMARILLO	(16) Dial 1030
D1071-C	RELAXIN' AT CAMARILLO	(16) Dial 1012
D1071-D	RELAXIN' AT CAMARILLO	(16) Dial LP901
D1071-E	RELAXIN' AT CAMARILLO	(16) Dial LP202
D1072-A	CHEERS	(16) Dial LP202
D1072-B	CHEERS	(16) Spotlite 103
D1072-D	CHEERS	(16) Spotlite 103
D1072-D	CHEERS	(16) Dial 1013
D1073-A	CARVIN' THE BIRD	(16) Dial LP901
D1073-B	CARVIN' THE BIRD	(16) Dial 1013
D1074-A	STUPENDOUS	(16) Dial 1022
D1074-B	STUPENDOUS	(16) Dial LP202

HOWARD McGHEE QUINTET

Howard McGhee (tp), Charlie Parker (as), Hampton Hawes (p), Addison Farmer (b), Roy Porter (d). *Hi-de-Ho Club, LA, March 9, 1947*

	DEE DEE'S DANCE	.	(15) Spotlite 107*

CHARLIE PARKER ALL STARS

Miles Davis (tp), Charlie Parker (as), Bud Powell (p), Tommy Potter (b), Max Roach (d). *NYC, May 8, 1947*

S3420-1	DONNA LEE	(3) Savoy S5J5500*
S3420-2	DONNA LEE	(3,4) Savoy MG12001
S3420-3	DONNA LEE	(3,4) Savoy MG12001
S3420-4	DONNA LEE	(3,5) Savoy MG12009
S3420-5	DONNA LEE	(3,6) Savoy 652
S3421-1	CHASIN' THE BIRD	(3,4) Savoy MG12001
S3421-2	CHASIN' THE BIRD	(3) Savoy S5J5500*
S3421-3	CHASIN' THE BIRD	(3,5) Savoy MG12009
S3421-4	CHASIN' THE BIRD	(3,6) Savoy 977
S3422-1	CHERYL	(3) Savoy MG12001*
S3422-2	CHERYL	(3,6) Savoy 952
S3423-1	BUZZY	(3,4) Dial MG12009
S3423-2	BUZZY	(3) Savoy MG12001*
S3423-3	BUZZY	(3,5) Savoy MG12001
S3423-4	BUZZY	(3) Savoy MG12000*
S3423-5	BUZZY	(3,6) Savoy 652

MILES DAVIS ALL STARS

Miles Davis (tp), Charlie Parker (ts), John Lewis (p), Nelson Boyd (b), Max Roach (d). *NYC, August 14, 1947*

S3440–1	MILESTONES	(3) Savoy S5J5500*
S3440–2	MILESTONES	(3,5) Savoy MG12009
S3440–3	MILESTONES	(3,6) Savoy 934
S3441–1	LITTLE WILLIE LEAPS	(3) Savoy MG12001*
S3441–2	LITTLE WILLIE LEAPS	(3,5) Savoy MG12001
S3441–3	LITTLE WILLIE LEAPS	(3,6) Savoy 977
S3442–1	HALF NELSON	(3,5) Savoy MG12001
S3442–2	HALF NELSON	(3,6) Savoy 951
S3443–1	SIPPIN' AT BELLS	(3) Savoy MG12009*
S3443–2	SIPPIN' AT BELLS	(3,6) Savoy 934
S3443–3	SIPPIN' AT BELLS	(3) Savoy S5J5500*
S3443–4	SIPPIN' AT BELLS	(3,5) Savoy MG12001

BARRY ULANOV'S ALL STAR MODERN JAZZ MUSICIANS

Dizzy Gillespie (tp), Charlie Parker (as), John LaPorta (cl), Lennie Tristano (p), Billy Bauer (g), Ray Brown (b), Max Roach (d). *NYC, September 13, 1947*

KOKO (THEME)	(15) Spotlite 107
HOT HOUSE	(15) Spotlite 107
I SURRENDER DEAR -1	(15) Spotlite 107
FINE AND DANDY	(15) Spotlite 107

NYC, September 20, 1947.

KOKO (THEME)	(15) Spotlite 107
ON THE SUNNY SIDE OF THE STREET	(15) Spotlite 107
HOW DEEP IS THE OCEAN	(15) Spotlite 107
TIGER RAG	(15) Steiner Davis 49
52ND STREET THEME (THEME)	(15) Spotlite 107

1- Gillespie, Parker and LaPorta out

"A NITE AT CARNEGIE HALL"

Dizzy Gillespie (tp), Charlie Parker (as), John Lewis (p), Al McKibbon (b), Joe Harris (d). *Carnegie Hall, NYC, September 29, 1947*

13000/1	NIGHT IN TUNISIA	(18) Black Deuce (unnumbered)
13002	DIZZY ATMOSPHERE	(18) Black Deuce
13003/4	GROOVIN' HIGH	(18) Black Deuce
13005	CONFIRMATION (RIFF WARMER)	(18) Black Deuce*
	KOKO	(18) Natural Organic 7000

CHARLIE PARKER QUINTET

Miles Davis (tp), Charlie Parker (as), Duke Jordan (p), Tommy Potter (b), Max Roach (d). *NYC, October 28, 1947*

D1101A	DEXTERITY	(19) Dial LP203
D1101B	DEXTERITY	(19) Dial 1032
D1102A	BONGO BOP (BLUES)	(19) Dial 1024
D1102B	BONGO BOP (PARKER'S BLUES)	(19) Dial 1024
D1103A	PREZOLOGY (DEWEY SQUARE)	(19) Dial 1056*
D1103B	DEWEY SQUARE	(19) Dial LP203
D1103C	DEWEY SQUARE	(19) Dial 1019
D1104A	THE HYMN (SUPERMAN)	(19) Dial 1056

D1104B	SUPERMAN	(19) Dial LP212
D1105A	BIRD OF PARADISE (ALL THE THINGS YOU ARE)	(19) Dial 1032
D1105B	BIRD OF PARADISE	(19) Dial 1032
D1105C	BIRD OF PARADISE	(19) Dial 1032
D1106A	EMBRACEABLE YOU	(19) Dial 1024
D1106B	EMBRACEABLE YOU	(19) Dial 1024

NYC, November 4, 1947.

D1111C	BIRD FEATHERS (SCHNOURPHOLOGY)	(20) Dial 1058
D1112A	KLACTOVEEDSEDSTENE	(20) Dial 1040
D1112B	KLACTOVEEDSEDSTENE	(20) Dial LP904
D1113B	SCRAPPLE FROM THE APPLE	(20) Dial LP203
D1113C	SCRAPPLE FROM THE APPLE	(20) Dial 1021
D1114A	MY OLD FLAME	(20) Dial 1058
D1115A	OUT OF NOWHERE	(20) Dial LP207
D1115B	OUT OF NOWHERE	(20) Dial LP904
D1115C	OUT OF NOWHERE	(20) Spotlite 105
D1116A	DON'T BLAME ME	(20) Dial 1021

BARRY ULANOV AND HIS ALL STAR METRONOME JAZZMEN

Fats Navarro (tp), Charlie Parker (as), Allen Eager (ts), John LaPorta (cl), Lennie Tristano (p), Billy Bauer (g), Tommy Potter (b), Buddy Rich (d), Sarah Vaughan (vcl). *NYC, November 8, 1947*

	52ND STREET THEME (THEME)	(21) Spotlite 108
	DONNA LEE -3,4	(21) Spotlite 108
	EVERYTHING I HAVE IS YOURS -1,2,3,4,vSV	(21) Spotlite 108
	FATS FLATS -3,4	(21) Spotlite 108
	TEA FOR TWO -1,2,3	(21) Spotlite 108
	DON'T BLAME ME -1,2,3,4,5	(21) Spotlite 108
	GROOVIN' HIGH	(21) Spotlite 108
	KOKO/ANTHROPOLOGY	(21) Spotlite 108

1- Navarro out, 2- Parker out, 3- Eager out, 4- LaPorta out, 5- Roach out.

CHARLIE PARKER SEXTET

As November 4 plus J. J. Johnson (tb). *NYC, December 17, 1947*

D1151B	GIANT SWING (DRIFTING ON A REED)	(22) Dial 1056
D1151D	DRIFTING ON A REED	(22) Dial LP904
D1151E	DRIFTING ON A REED (AIR CONDITIONING)	(22) Dial 1043
D1152A	QUASIMODO	(22) Dial LP203
D1152B	QUASIMODO (TRADE WINDS)	(22) Dial 1015
D1153B	CHARLIE'S WIG	(22) Dial LP203
D1153D	BONGO BOP (CHARLIE'S WIG)	(22) Dial LP203
D1153E	CHARLIE'S WIG	(22) Dial 1040
D1154B	DEXTERITY (BIRD FEATHERS)	(22) Dial LP904
D1154C	BIRD FEATHERS (BONGO BEEP)	(22) Dial LP207
D1155ABX	CRAZEOLOGY II	(22) Dial 1034**
D1155C	CRAZEOLOGY	(22) Dial LP905
D1155D	CRAZEOLOGY	(22) Dial 1034, 1055
D1156A	HOW DEEP IS THE OCEAN	(22) Dial 1055
D1156B	HOW DEEP IS THE OCEAN	(22) Dial LP211

CHARLIE PARKER ALL STARS

As last except Johnson out. *Detroit, December 21, 1947*

D830-1	ANOTHER HAIR-DO	(3) Savoy MG12000*
D830-2	ANOTHER HAIR-DO	(3) Savoy MG12000*
D830-3	ANOTHER HAIR-DO	(3) Savoy S5J5500*
D830-4	ANOTHER HAIR-DO	(3,6) Savoy 961
D831-1	BLUEBIRD	(3,5) Savoy MG12000
D831-2	BLUEBIRD	(3) Savoy S5J5500*
D831-3	BLUEBIRD	(3,6) Savoy 961
D832-1	KLAUNSEN'S VANSEN'S (KLAUNSTANCE)	(3,6) Savoy 967
D833-1	BIRD GETS THE WORM	(3,5)) Savoy MG12000
D833-2	BIRD GETS THE WORM	(3) Savoy S5J5500*
D833-3	BIRD GETS THE WORM	(3,6) Savoy 952

CHARLIE PARKER QUINTET

As last plus Kenny Hagood (vcl). *Three Deuces, NYC, c. March, 1948*

	DIZZY ATMOSPHERE	(23) Spotlite SPJ141
	MY OLD FLAME	(23) Spotlite SPJ141*
	ALL THE THINGS YOU ARE vKH	(23) Spotlite SPJ141*
	HALF NELSON	(23) Spotlite SPJ141*
	DRIFTING ON A REED (BIG FOOT)	(23) Spotlite SPJ141
	52ND STREET THEME (3 VERSIONS)	(23) Spotlite SPJ141

Onyx Club, NYC, c. Spring 1948.

	52ND STREET THEME	(24) Jazz Workshop JWS501**
	SHAW NUFF	(24) Jazz Workshop JWS501**
	OUT OF NOWHERE	(24) Jazz Workshop JWS501**
	HOT HOUSE	(24) Jazz Workshop JWS501**
	THIS TIME THE DREAM'S ON ME	(24) Jazz Workshop JWS501**
	NIGHT IN TUNISIA	(24) Jazz Workshop JWS501*
	MY OLD FLAME	(24) Jazz Workshop JWS501**
	52ND STREET THEME (2 VERSIONS)	(24) Jazz Workshop JWS501*
	THE WAY YOU LOOK TONIGHT	(24) Jazz Workshop JWS501**
	OUT OF NOWHERE	(24) Jazz Workshop JWS501**
	CHASIN' THE BIRD	(24) Jazz Workshop JWS501*
	THIS TIME THE DREAM'S ON ME	(24) Jazz Workshop JWS501
	DIZZY ATMOSPHERE	(24) Jazz Workshop JWS501**
	HOW HIGH THE MOON	(24) Jazz Workshop JWS501**

CHARLIE PARKER ALL STARS

As last except Tadd Dameron (p), Curley Russell (b) replace Jordan and Potter. *Royal Roost, NYC, September 4, 1948.*

	52ND STREET THEME	(25) Savoy MG12186
	KOKO	(25,26) Le Jazz Cool LJC101

As last except John Lewis (p) replaces Dameron. *NYC, September 18, 1948.*

B900-1	BARBADOS	(3) Savoy MG12000
B900-2	BARBADOS	(3) Savoy MG12009*
B900-3	BARBADOS	(3,5) Savoy MG12009
B900-4	BARBADOS	(3,6) Savoy 936
B901-1	AH-LEU-CHA	(3) Savoy MG12000*
B901-2	AH-LEU-CHA	(3,6) Savoy 939
B902-1	CONSTELLATION	(3) Savoy S5J5500*
B902-2	CONSTELLATION	(3) Savoy MG12000
B902-3	CONSTELLATION	(3) Savoy MG12000*
B902-4	CONSTELLATION	(3) Savoy MG12009*
B902-5	CONSTELLATION	(3,6) Savoy 939
B903-1	PARKER'S MOOD -1	(3) Savoy S5J5500*
B903-2	PARKER'S MOOD -1	(3,4) Savoy MG12000
B903-3	PARKER'S MOOD -1	(3) Savoy S5J5500*
B903-4	PARKER'S MOOD -1	(3) Savoy MG12009*
B903-5	PARKER'S MOOD -1	(3,6) Savoy 936

NYC, September 24, 1948.

B908-1	PERHAPS	(3,4) Savoy MG12014
B908-2	PERHAPS	(3) Savoy MG12009*
B908-3	PERHAPS	(3,4) Savoy MG12009
B908-4	PERHAPS	(3) Savoy S5J5500*
B908-5	PERHAPS	(3) Savoy MG12000*
B908-6	PERHAPS	(3,4) Savoy MG12000
B908-7	PERHAPS	(3,6) Savoy 938
B909-1	MARMADUKE	(3) Savoy S5J5500*
B909-2	MARMADUKE	(3) Savoy MG12000*
B909-3	MARMADUKE	(3) Savoy S5J5500*
B909-4	MARMADUKE	(3) Savoy S5J5500*
B909-5	MARMADUKE	(3,4) Savoy MG12000
B909-6	MARMADUKE	(3,4) Savoy SJL1129*
B909-7	MARMADUKE	(3,4) Savoy MG12001*
B909-8	MARMADUKE	(3,4) Savoy MG12001*
B909-9	MARMADUKE	(3,4) Savoy MG12001
B909-10	MARMADUKE	(3) Savoy S5J5500*
B909-11	MARMADUKE	(3) Savoy MG12009*
B909-12	MARMADUKE	(3,6) Savoy 938
B910-1	STEEPLECHASE	(3) Savoy S5J5500*
B910-2	STEEPLECHASE	(3,6) Savoy 937
B911-1	MERRY-GO-ROUND	(3) Savoy MG12000
B911-2	MERRY-GO-ROUND	(3,6) Savoy 937

1- Davis out.

CHARLIE PARKER WITH THE NEAL HEFTI ORCHESTRA

Charlie Parker (as) with Al Porcino, Ray Wetzel, Doug Mettome (tp), Bill Harris, Bart Varsalona (tb), Vincent Jacobs (fr-h), Murray Williams, Sonny Salad (as),

Flip Phillips, Pete Mondello (ts), John LaPorta (cl), Sam Caplan, Harry Katzman, Gene Orloff, Ziggy Smirnoff, Sid Harris, Manny Fidler (vln), Joe Benaventi (cel), Tony Aless (p), Curley Russell (b), Shelly Manne (d), Diego Iborra (cga, bgo), Neal Hefti (arr, cond). *NYC, Autumn 1948*

| 2071-5 | REPETITION | (27) Jazz Scene |
| | | (unnumbered) |

Note: It is possible that the orchestra was recorded in late 1947 and Parker overdubbed the following autumn.

CHARLIE PARKER ALL STARS

Miles Davis (tp), Charlie Parker (as, vcl), Al Haig (p), Tommy Potter (b), Max Roach (d). *Royal Roost, NYC, December 11, 1948.*

	GROOVIN' HIGH	(26,28) Le Jazz Cool
		LJC101**
	DRIFTING ON A REED (BIG FOOT)	(28) Le Jazz Cool
		LJC102
	ORNITHOLOGY	(28,29) Le Jazz Cool
		LJC101**
	SLOW BOAT TO CHINA	(28) ESP ESP-BIRD-1

Royal Roost, NYC, December 12, 1948.

	HOT HOUSE	(30) Le Jazz Cool
		LJC101**, LJC103
	SALT PEANUTS vCP	(29) Le Jazz Cool
		LJC102

Royal Roost, NYC, December 18, 1948.

	CHASIN' THE BIRD	Meexa Discox 1776
	OUT OF NOWHERE	(29) Le Jazz Cool
		LJC102
	HOW HIGH THE MOON	(26) Le Jazz Cool
		LJC102

MACHITO AND HIS ORCHESTRA

Charlie Parker (as) with Mario Bauza, Paquito Davilla, Bob Woodlen (tp), Gene Johnson, Freddie Skerritt (as), Jose Madera (ts), Leslie Johnakins (bs), Rene Hernandez (p), Roberto Rodriguez (b), Jose Mangual (bgo), Luis Miranda (cga), Ubaldo Nieto (tbl), Machito (mca), band vcl. *NYC, December 20, 1948*

| 2155-2 | NO NOISE PT. 2 | (31) Mercury/Clef 11012 |
| 2157-1 | MANGO MANGUE v | (31) Mercury/Clef 11017 |

CHARLIE PARKER ALL STARS

As December 11 except Kenny Dorham (tp) replaces Davis. *Royal Roost, NYC, December 25, 1948*

	HALF NELSON	(28) Okiedoke
		(unnumbered)
	WHITE CHRISTMAS	(26, 28) Le Jazz Cool
		LJC101**
	LITTLE WILLIE LEAPS	(28) Okiedoke

As last except Joe Harris (d) replaces Roach. *Royal Roost, NYC, January 1, 1949.*

	BEBOP	(25) ESP ESP-BIRD-2
	SLOW BOAT TO CHINA	(25,30) Le Jazz Cool
		LJC103
	ORNITHOLOGY	(25) ESP ESP-BIRD-2

GROOVIN' HIGH	(25) ESP ESP-BIRD-2
EAST OF THE SUN	(25) ESP ESP-BIRD-2
CHERYL	(25,30) Le Jazz Cool LJC102**

METRONOME ALL STARS

Dizzy Gillespie, Fats Navarro, Miles Davis (tp), J. J. Johnson, Kai Winding (tb), Charlie Parker (as), Charlie Ventura (ts), Ernie Caceres (bs), Buddy DeFranco (cl), Lennie Tristano (p, arr -1), Billy Bauer (g), Eddie Safranski (b), Shelly Manne (d), Pete Rugolo (cond, arr-2). *NYC, January 3, 1949*

D9-VB-0021-1	OVERTIME -2	Victor 20-3361
D9-VC-1000-2	OVERTIME -2	(32) Victor EPBT3046
D9-VB-0022-1	VICTORY BALL -1,3	Victor 20-3361
D9-VB-0022-2	VICTORY BALL -1,3	Camden CAL339
D9-VC-1001-3	VICTORY BALL -1	(32) Victor EPBT3046

3- Navarro, Davis, Johnson and Caceres out.

CHARLIE PARKER ALL STARS

As January 1. *Royal Roost, NYC, January 15, 1949*

SCRAPPLE FROM THE APPLE	(30) Le Jazz Cool LJC103
BEBOP	(30) Le Jazz Cool LJC103
HOT HOUSE	(29) Le Jazz Cool LJC103

Max Roach (d) replaces Harris. *Royal Roost, NYC, January 22, 1949.*

OOP BOP SH'BAM vCP	(30) Le Jazz Cool LJC103
SCRAPPLE FROM THE APPLE	Grotto 495
SALT PEANUTS vCP	Grotto 495

MACHITO AND HIS ORCHESTRA WITH CHARLIE PARKER

As December 20. *NYC, January 1949*

2171-1	OKIEDOKE	(31) Mercury/Clef 11017

CHARLIE PARKER ALL STARS

As January 22. *Royal Roost, NYC, February 5, 1949*

BARBADOS	(30) Le Jazz Cool LJC103
SALT PEANUTS vCP	(30) Le Jazz Cool LJC103

Royal Roost, NYC, February 12, 1949.

SCRAPPLE FROM THE APPLE	(33) Savoy SJL1108
BARBADOS	(33) Savoy MG12179
BEPOP	(33) Savoy SJL1108
GROOVIN' HIGH	(29,33) Le Jazz Cool LJC103
CONFIRMATION	(33) Savoy SJL1108
SALT PEANUTS vCP	(33) Savoy SJL1108
JUMPIN' WITH SYMPHONY SID (THEME)	(33) Savoy SJL1108

CHARLIE PARKER

Charlie Parker (as), Hank Jones (p), Ray Brown (b), Shelly Manne (d). *NYC, February 1949*

2081-5   THE BIRD   (27) Jazz Scene
                                                  (unnumbered)

CHARLIE PARKER ALL STARS

As February 19 plus Lucky Thompson (ts), Milt Jackson (vib), Dave Lambert,
Buddy Stewart (vcl). *Royal Roost, NYC, February 26, 1949*

                  HALF NELSON   (33) Savoy MG12179
                  NIGHT IN TUNISIA   (33) Savoy MG12186
                  SCRAPPLE FROM THE APPLE   (33) Savoy MG12179
                  DEEDLE vDL, BS -1,2   Grotto 495
                  WHAT THIS? vDL, BS -1,2   S.C.A.M. JPG3

Royal Roost, NYC, March 5, 1949

                  DEEDLE vDL, BS -1,2   Grotto 495
                  ROYAL ROOST BOP vDL, BS -1,2   Grotto 495
                  CHERYL   S.C.A.M. JPG3
                  ANTHROPOLOGY   S.C.A.M. JPG3

Waldorf Astoria, NYC, March 5, 1949.

                  BARBADOS -2   Jazz Showcase 5003
                  ANTHROPOLOGY   (34) Jazz Showcase 5003

Royal Roost, NYC, March 12, 1949.

                  CHERYL   (33) Savoy MG12179
                  SLOW BOAT TO CHINA -1   (33) Savoy MG12179
                  CHASING THE BIRD   (33) Savoy MG12179

1- Thompson out, 2- Jackson out.

CHARLIE PARKER AND HIS ORCHESTRA

As February 26 except Tommy Turk (tb), Carlos Vidal (bgo) replace Thompson
and Jackson. *NYC, April 1949*

292   CARDBOARD   (27) Norgran MGN1035
293   VISA   (27) Mercury/Clef 11022

Turk and Vidal out. *NYC, May 5, 1949.*

294-3   SEGMENT   (27) Verve MGV8009
295-2   PASSPORT   (27) Mercury/Clef 11022
295-5   PASSPORT   Verve MGV8000
296   DIVERSE (actually SEGMENT!)   Verve MGV8009

Salle Pleyel, Paris, May 8/9/14/15, 1949.

                  SALT PEANUTS vCP   (35) Bird in Paris CP3
                  BARBADOS   (35) Bird in Paris CP3*
                  52ND STREET THEME   (35) Bird in Paris CP3
                  OUT OF NOWHERE   (35) Bird in Paris CP3
                  SALT PEANUTS vCP   (35) Bird in Paris CP3
                  SCRAPPLE FROM THE APPLE   (35) Bird in Paris CP3
                  OUT OF NOWHERE   (35) Bird in Paris CP3*
                  ALLEN'S ALLEY   (35) Bird in Paris CP3*
                  52ND STREET THEME   (35) Bird in Paris CP3*
                  HAM AND HAIG (i.e. HOT HOUSE)   Vogue V5012*

JAM SESSION

Hot Lips Page, Miles Davis, Bill Coleman, Aime Barelli (tp), Russell Moore (tb),
Sidney Bechet, Pierre Braslavsky (ss), Charlie Parker (as), Don Byas, James

Moody (ts), Hubert Rostaing (cl), Al Haig (p), Hazy Osterwald (vib), Toots Thielmans (g), Tommy Potter (b), Max Roach (d). *Salle Pleyel, Paris, May 15, 1949*

	FAREWELL BLUES	(35) Bird in Paris CP3*

JAZZ AT THE PHILHARMONIC

Roy Eldridge (tp), Tommy Turk (tb), Charlie Parker (as), Lester Young, Flip Phillips (ts), Hank Jones (p), Ray Brown (b), Buddy Rich (d), Ella Fitzgerald (vcl). *Carnegie Hall, NYC, September 18, 1949*

382/3/4	THE OPENER	(35a) Mercury/Clef 11054/5/6
385/6/7	LESTER LEAPS IN	(35a) Mercury/Clef 11056/5/4
	EMBRACEABLE YOU	(35a) Mercury MG35013
	THE CLOSER	(35a) Mercury MG35013
	FLYING HOME vEF	(35b) Verve 815.147

CHARLIE PARKER WITH STRINGS

Charlie Parker (as), Mitch Miller (ob, eng-h), Bronislaw Gimpel, Max Hollander, Milton Lamask (vln), Frank Briett (vla), Frank Miller (cel), Meyer Rosen (harp), Stan Freeman (p), Ray Brown (b), Buddy Rich (d), Jimmy Carroll (arr, cond). *NYC, November 30, 1949*

319–5	JUST FRIENDS	(27) Mercury/Clef 11036
320–3	EVERYTHING HAPPENS TO ME	(27) Mercury/Clef 11036
321–3	APRIL IN PARIS	(27) Mercury/Clef 11037
322–2	SUMMERTIME	(27) Mercury/Clef 11038
323–2	I DIDN'T KNOW WHAT TIME IT WAS	(27) Mercury/Clef 11038
324–2	IF I SHOULD LOSE YOU	(27) Mercury/Clef 11037

CHARLIE PARKER QUINTET

Red Rodney (tp), Charlie Parker (as), Al Haig (p), Tommy Potter (b), Roy Haynes (d). *Carnegie Hall, NYC, December 24, 1949*

	ORNITHOLOGY	(36) Hot Club de Lyon
	CHERYL	(36) Hot Club de Lyon
	KOKO	(36) Hot Club de Lyon
	BIRD OF PARADISE (BIRD'S PERCH)	(36) Hot Club de Lyon
	NOW'S THE TIME	(36) Hot Club de Lyon

CHARLIE PARKER

Charlie Parker (as), Teddy Wilson (p), Eddie Safranski (b), Don Lamond (d). *Brooklyn, NYC, 1949*

	COOL BLUES	(36) Jazz Showcase 5003

Bernie Leighton (p), Ray Brown (b), Buddy Rich (d) replace Wilson, Safranski and Lamond. *Probably NYC, 1950.*

	I CAN'T GET STARTED	(36) Parktec 4627–1

CHARLIE PARKER

As December 24 plus J. J. Johnson (tb). *Birdland, NYC, February 14, 1950.*

	ANTHROPOLOGY/ALLEN'S ALLEY	(37) J for Jazz JFJ802
	VISA/52ND STREET THEME	(37) J for Jazz JFJ802
	DIZZY ATMOSPHERE	(38) Chazzer 2001*
	YESTERDAYS/52ND STREET THERE	(38) Chazzer 2001*

Johnson out. *St. Nicholas Arena, NYC, February 18, 1950.*

	I DIDN'T KNOW WHAT TIME IT WAS	(39) Jazz Workshop JWS500**
	ORNITHOLOGY	(39) Jazz Workshop JWS500**
	EMBRACEABLE YOU	(39) Jazz Workshop JWS500**
	VISA	(39) Jazz Workshop JWS500**
	I COVER THE WATERFRONT	(39) Jazz Workshop JWS500**
	SCRAPPLE FROM THE APPLE	(39) Jazz Workshop JWS500**
	STAR EYES/52ND STREET THEME	(39) Jazz Workshop JWS500**
	CONFIRMATION	(39) Jazz Workshop JWS500**
	OUT OF NOWHERE	(39) Jazz Workshop JWS500**
	HOT HOUSE	(39) Jazz Workshop JWS500**
	WHAT'S NEW	(39) Jazz Workshop JWS500**
	NOW'S THE TIME	(39) Jazz Workshop JWS500**
	SMOKE GETS IN YOUR EYES/52ND STREET THEME	(39) Jazz Workshop JWS500**

Charlie Parker (as), Hank Jones (p), Ray Brown (b), Buddy Rich (d). *NYC, March-April 1950.*

371–4	STAR EYES	(27) Norgran MGN1035
372–12	BLUES (FAST)	(27) Verve MGV8009
373–2	I'M IN THE MOOD FOR LOVE	(27) Verve MGV8009

As last plus Coleman Hawkins (ts -1). *Possible LA(?) same period.*

	CELEBRITY	(27) Verve MGV8002
	BALLADE -1	(27) Verve MGV8002

GENE ROLAND ORCHESTRA

Marty Bell, Don Ferrara, Don Joseph, Jon Nielson, Al Porcino, Sonny Rich, Red Rodney, Bill Verlin (tp), Eddie Bert, Porky Cohen, Jimmy Knepper, Paul Selden (tb), Frank Orchard (vtb), Charlie Parker, Joe Maini (as), Al Cohn, Don Lanphere, Tommy Mackagon, Zoot Sims (ts), Bob Newman, prob. Marty Flax (bs), unknown p, Sam Herman (g), Buddy Jones (b), Artie Anton, poss. Tiny Kahn (d), Gene Roland (arr, cond), *NYC, April 3, 1950*

	IT'S A WONDERFUL WORLD	(23) Spotlite SPJ141*
	JUST YOU, JUST ME	(23) Spotlite SPJ141*
	UNKNOWN TITLE	(23) Spotlite SPJ141*
	STARDUST	(23) Spotlite SPJ141*

CHARLIE PARKER

With unknown Latin band. *Renaissance Ballroom, NYC, c. May 1950*

	BONGO BALLAD (MAMBO FORTUNADO)	(40) Jazz Showcase 5003
	BIRD'S MAMBO (LAMENT FOR THE CONGA)	(40) Jazz Showcase 5003

CHARLIE PARKER QUINTET

As February 18. *Cafe Society, NYC, May 1950*

JUST FRIENDS (2 VERSIONS)	(41) Grotto 495
APRIL IN PARIS (2 VERSIONS)	(41) Grotto 495
NIGHT IN TUNISIA	(41) Grotto 495
MOOSE THE MOOCHE -1	(41) Bombasi 11235

Kenny Dorham (tp) replaces Rodney. *Cafe Society, NYC, May 23, 1950*

BEWITCHED/SUMMERTIME/I COVER THE WATERFRONT/EASY TO LOVE /52ND STREET THEME	Klacto MG101

Cafe Society, NYC, same period.

52ND STREET THEME	Klacto MG101
JUST FRIENDS	Klacto MG101
APRIL IN PARIS	Klacto MG101

1- Tony Scott (cl) added

CHARLIE PARKER AND HIS ORCHESTRA

Dizzy Gillespie (tp), Charlie Parker (as), Thelonious Monk (p), Curley Russell (b), Buddy Rich (d). *NYC, June 6, 1950*

410-4	BLOOMDIDO	(27) Mercury/Clef 11058
411-3	AN OSCAR FOR TREADWELL	(27) Verve MGV8006
411-4	AN OSCAR FOR TREADWELL	Mercury/Clef 11082
412-3	MOHAWK	(27) Verve MGV8006
412-6	MOHAWK	Mercury/Clef 11082
413-2	MY MELANCHOLY BABY	(27) Mercury/Clef 11058
414-4	LEAP FROG	(27) Verve MGV 8006
414-6	LEAP FROG	(27) Mercury/Clef 11076
415-2	RELAXIN' WITH LEE	(27) Verve MGV8006
415-3	RELAXIN' WITH LEE	Mercury/Clef 11076

Fats Navarro (tp), Charlie Parker (as), Bud Powell (p), Curley Russell (b), Art Blakey (d). *Birdland, NYC, June 30, 1950.*

WAHOO (PERDIDO)	(42) Le Jazz Cool LJC102**
'ROUND MIDNIGHT -1	(26,42) Le Jazz Cool LJC101
THIS TIME THE DREAM'S ON ME -1	(42) Columbia JG34808
DIZZY ATMOSPHERE	(42) Columbia JG34808
NIGHT IN TUNISIA -2	(42) Columbia JG34808
MOVE	(26,42) Le Jazz Cool LJC101**
THE STREET BEAT (RIFFTIDE)	(42) Le Jazz Cool LJC102
OUT OF NOWHERE	(42) Columbia JG34808
LITTLE WILLIE LEAPS/52ND STREET THEME	(42) Meexa Discox 1776
ORNITHOLOGY	(42) Le Jazz Cool LJC101
I'LL REMEMBER APRIL/52ND STREET THEME	(42) Grotto 495

Walter Bishop (p) replaces Powell. *Same location and date.*

EMBRACEABLE YOU -3	(42) Meexa Discox 1776

COOL BLUES/52ND STREET THEME	(26,42) Le Jazz Cool
	LJC 101*
CONCEPTION (POOBAH) -4	Alto AL701

1- Navarro out, 2- Parker out, 3- Chubby Newsome (vcl) added, 4- Miles Davis (tp), J. J. Johnson (tb), Brew Moore (ts) added while Navarro and Parker play only in final ensemble.

CHARLIE PARKER

Norma Carson, Jon Eardley (tp), Jimmy Knepper (tb), Charlie Parker, Joe Maini (as), Bob Newman, Gers Yowell (ts), John Williams (p), Buddy Jones (b), Phil Brown -1, Frank Isola -2, Buzzy Bridgeford -3 (d). *NYC, c. June 1950*

LITTLE WILLIE LEAPS -1	(43) Zim ZM1006**
ALL THE THINGS YOU ARE -2	(43) Zim ZM1006**
BERNIE'S TUNE -3	(43) Zim ZM1006**
DONNA LEE -1	(43) Zim ZM1006**
OUT OF NOWHERE -2	(43) Zim ZM1006**
HALF NELSON -1	(43) Zim ZM1006**
FINE AND DANDY -1	(43) Zim ZM1006**

Similar, poss. incl. Jon Nielson (tp), Don Lanphere (ts). *Same period.*

HALF NELSON	(43) Zim ZM1006**
CHEROKEE	(43) Zim ZM1006**
SCRAPPLE FROM THE APPLE	(43) Zim ZM1006**
STAR EYES	(43) Zim ZM1006**

Charlie Parker (as), Brew Moore (ts), Tony Scott (cl), Dick Hyman (p), poss. Chuck Wayne (g), Leonard Gaskin (b), Irv Kluger (d). *Cafe Society, NYC, June/July 1950.*

| LOVER COME BACK TO ME/52ND | (41) Parktec 4627-1 |
| STREET THEME | |

CHARLIE PARKER WITH STRINGS

Joseph Singer (fr-h), Charlie Parker (as), Edwin Brown (ob), Sam Caplan, Howard Kay, Sam Rand, Harry Melnikoff, Zelly Smirnoff (vln), Isadore Zir (vla), Maurice Brown (cel), Verley Mills (harp), Bernie Leighton (p), Ray Brown (b), Buddy Rich (d), Joe Lippman (arr, cond). *NYC, July 5, 1950*

442-5	DANCING IN THE DARK	(44) Mercury/Clef 11068
443-2	OUT OF NOWHERE	(44) Mercury/Clef 11070
444-3	LAURA	(44) Mercury/Clef 11068
445-4	EAST OF THE SUN	(44) Mercury/Clef 11070
446-2	THEY CAN'T TAKE THAT AWAY	(44) Mercury/Clef 11071
447-4	EASY TO LOVE	(44) Mercury/Clef 11072
448-2	I'M IN THE MOOD FOR LOVE	(44) Mercury/Clef 11071
449-2	I'LL REMEMBER APRIL	(44) Mercury/Clef 11072

Similar to next session. *Apollo Theatre, NYC, August 23, 1950.*

EASY TO LOVE	(41,45) S.C.A.M. JPG4
REPETITION	(30) Saga ERO8006
APRIL IN PARIS	(30) Saga ERO8006
WHAT IS THIS THING CALLED LOVE	(30) Saga ERO8006

Charlie Parker (as), Tommy Mace (ob), Sam Caplan, Stan Karpenia, Teddy Blume (vln), Dave Uchitel (vla), Bill Bundy (cel), Wallace McManus (harp), Al Haig (p), Tommy Potter (b), Roy Haynes (d), Jimmy Mundy -1, Gerry Mulligan -2 (arr). *Carnegie Hall, NYC, September 16, 1950.*

REPETITION	(44) Norgran MGJC3502
WHAT IS THIS THING CALLED LOVE	(44) Norgran MGJC3502
APRIL IN PARIS	(44) Norgran MGJC3502
EASY TO LOVE -1	(44) Norgran MGJC3502
ROCKER (I'LL REMEMBER APRIL) -2	(44) Norgran MGJC3502

CHARLIE PARKER

Charlie Parker (as), Claude McLin (ts), Chris Anderson (p), George Freeman (g), Leroy Jackson (b), Bruz Freeman (d), unknown vcl. *Pershing Ballroom, Chicago, autumn 1950*

THERE'S A SMALL HOTEL	(46) Savoy MG12152
THESE FOOLISH THINGS	(46) Savoy MG12152*
KEEN AND PEACHY	(46) Savoy MG12152*
HOT HOUSE	(46) Savoy MG12152*
BIRD, BASS AND OUT	(46) Savoy SJL1132*
GOODBYE	(46) Savoy SJL1132*
INDIANA	(47) Zim ZM1003**
I CAN'T GET STARTED	(47) Zim ZM1003**
ANTHROPOLOGY	(47) Zim ZM1003**
OUT OF NOWHERE	(47) Zim ZM1003**
GET HAPPY	(47) Zim ZM1003**
HOT HOUSE	(47) Zim ZM1003**
EMBRACEABLE YOU v	(47) Zim ZM1003*
BODY AND SOUL v	(47) Zim ZM1003*
COOL BLUES	(47) Zim ZM1003**
STARDUST v	(47) Zim ZM1003**
ALL THE THINGS YOU ARE	(47) Zim ZM1003*
BILLIE'S BOUNCE	(47) Zim ZM1003**
PENNIES FROM HEAVEN	(47) Zim ZM1003**

Rolf Ericson (tp), Charlie Parker (as), Gosta Theselius (p -1, ts -2), Thore Jederby (b), Jack Noren (d). *Amiralen Dance Hall, Malmo, November 22, 1950*

ANTHROPOLOGY -1	(48) Oktav OKTLP164
CHEERS -1	(48) Oktav OKTLP164
LOVER MAN -1	(48) Oktav OKTLP164
COOL BLUES -1	(48) Oktav OKTLP164

Same. *Folkets Park, Halsingborg, November 24, 1950*

ANTHROPOLOGY -1	(48) Sonet SLP27
SCRAPPLE FROM THE APPLE -1	(48) Sonet SLP27
EMBRACEABLE YOU -1	(48) Sonet SLP27
COOL BLUES -1	(48) Sonet SLP27
STAR EYES -1,3	(48) Sonet SLP27
ALL THE THINGS YOU ARE -1	(48) Sonet SLP27
STRIKE UP THE BAND -1	(48) Sonet SLP27

Rowland Greenberg (tp), Lennart Nilsson (p) added. *Same date.*

BODY AND SOUL -2	(48) Sonet SLP27
FINE AND DANDY -2	(48) Sonet SLP27
HOW HIGH THE MOON -2	(48) Sonet SLP27

3- Ericson out

Probably Roger Guerin, Georges Jouvin, unknown (tp), Andre Paquinet, Maurice Gladieu, unknown (tb), unknown ss, Charlie Parker, Robert Merchez (as), Roger Simon (ts), Honore True (bs), Robert Cambier (p), Henri Karen (b), Pierre Loteguy (d), unknown perc, Maurice Moufflard (cond). *Paris, November 1950.*

	LADY BIRD	(35) Bird in Paris CP3

MACHITO AND HIS ORCHESTRA
As December 20, 1948, plus Harry Edison, Al Stewart (tp), Flip Phillips (ts), Sol Rabinowitz (bs), Buddy Rich (d), Chino Pozo (cga), Chico O'Farrill (arr, cond). *NYC, December 21, 1950*

558-2	MAMBO	(31) Clef MGC505
559	RUMBA ABIERTA	(31) Clef MGC505
560-2	6/8	(31) Clef MGC505
561-3	JAZZ	(31) Clef MGC505

CHARLIE PARKER AND HIS ORCHESTRA
Miles Davis (tp), Charlie Parker (as), Walter Bishop (p), Teddy Kotick (b), Max Roach (d). *NYC, January 17, 1951*

489-2	AU PRIVAVE	(44) Verve MGV8010
489-3	AU PRIVAVE	Mercury/Clef 11087
490-3	SHE ROTE	(44) Verve MGV8010
490-5	SHE ROTE	Clef 11101
491-1	K.C. BLUES	(44) Clef 11101
492-2	STAR EYES	(44) Mercury/Clef 11087

CHARLIE PARKER AND HIS JAZZERS
Roy Haynes (d), Jose Mangual (bgo), Luis Miranda (cga) replace Davis and Roach. *NYC, March 12, 1951*

540-6	MY LITTLE SUEDE SHOES	(44) Mercury/Clef 11093
541-2	UN POQUITO DE TU AMOR	(44) Mercury/Clef 11092
542-9	TICO TICO	(44) Mercury/Clef 11091
543-3	FIESTA	(44) Norgram MGN1035
544-2	WHY DO I LOVE YOU	(44) Verve MGV8008
544-6	WHY DO I LOVE YOU	(44) Verve MGV8008
544-7	WHY DO I LOVE YOU	Clef MGC646

CHARLIE PARKER WITH STRINGS
Unknown ob and strings replace Mangual and Miranda. *Birdland, NYC, March 24, 1951*

	JUMPIN' WITH SYMPHONY SID (THEME)	(45) Columbia JC34832
	JUST FRIENDS	(45) Columbia JC34832
	EVERYTHING HAPPENS TO ME	(45) Columbia JC34832
	EAST OF THE SUN	(45) Columbia JC34832
	LAURA	(45) Columbia JC34832
	DANCING IN THE DARK	(45) Columbia JC34832
	JUMPIN' WITH SYMPHONY SID (THEME)	(45) Columbia JC34832

CHARLIE PARKER/DIZZY GILLESPIE

Dizzy Gillespie (tp), Charlie Parker (as), Bud Powell (p), Tommy Potter (b), Roy Haynes (d). *Birdland, NYC, March 31, 1951*

BLUE 'N BOOGIE	(49) Temple M555
ANTHROPOLOGY	(49) Temple M555
'ROUND MIDNIGHT	(49) Temple M555
NIGHT IN TUNISIA	(49) Temple M555
JUMPIN' WITH SYMPHONY SID (THEME)	(49) Temple M555

CHARLIE PARKER WITH STRINGS

As March 24. *Birdland, NYC, April 7, 1951*

WHAT IS THIS THING CALLED LOVE	(45) Columbia JC34832
LAURA	(45) Okiedoke
REPETITION	(45) Columbia JC34832
THEY CAN'T TAKE THAT AWAY	(45) Columbia JC34832
EASY TO LOVE	(45) Columbia JC34832

CHARLIE PARKER

Charlie Parker (as), Wardell Gray (ts), Walter Bishop, Nat Pierce (p), Teddy Kotick (b), Roy Haynes (d). *Christy's, Framingham, Mass., April 12, 1951*

SCRAPPLE FROM THE APPLE	Charlie Parker PLP404
LULLABY IN RHYTHM (I MAY BE WRONG)	Charlie Parker PLP404
HAPPY BIRD BLUES	Charlie Parker PLP404*

Charlie Parker (as), unknown (tp, ts) Dick Twardzik (p), Charles Mingus (b), unknown d. *Same location, c. summer 1951*

I'LL REMEMBER APRIL	(50) Charlie Parker PLP404

CHARLIE PARKER QUINTET

Red Rodney (tp), Charlie Parker (as), John Lewis (p), Ray Brown (b), Kenny Clarke (d). *NYC, August 8, 1951*

609-4	BLUES FOR ALICE (originally SI SI!)	(44) Clef MGC646
610-4	SI SI	(44) Mercury/Clef 11103
611-3	SWEDISH SCHNAPPS	(44) Verve MGV8010
611-4	SWEDISH SCHNAPPS	Mercury/Clef 11103
612-1	BACK HOME BLUES	(44) Verve MGV8010
612-2	BACK HOME BLUES	Mercury/Clef 11095
613-2	LOVERMAN	(44) VEVC MEV 8010 Mercury/Clef 11095

WOODY HERMAN AND HIS ORCHESTRA WITH CHARLIE PARKER

Charlie Parker (as) with Roy Caton, Don Fagerquist, Johnny Macombe, Doug Mettome (tp), Jerry Dorn, Urbie Green, Fred Lewis (tb), Dick Hafer, Bill Perkins, Kenny Pinson (ts), Sam Staff (bs), Dave McKenna (p), Red Wooten (b), Sonny Igoe (d), band vcl. *St. Louis, August 1951*

YOU GO TO MY HEAD	(51) MainMan BFWHCB617
LEO THE LION (THE LION)	(51) MainMan BFWHCB617
CUBAN HOLIDAY (CUBOP HOLIDAY)	(51) MainMan BFWHCB617

THE NEARNESS OF YOU		(51) MainMan
		BFWHCB617
LEMON DROP v		(51) MainMan
		BFWHCB617
THE GOOF AND I (SONNY SPEAKS)		(51) MainMan
		BFWHCB617
LAURA		(51) MainMan
		BFWHCB617
FOUR BROTHERS		(51) MainMan
		BFWHCB617
LEO THE LION		(51) Alamac QSR2442

CHARLIE PARKER/DIZZY GILLESPIE

Dizzy Gillespie (tp), Charlie Parker (as), Dick Hyman (p), Sandy Block (b), Charlie Smith (d). *NYC, early 1952*

	HOT HOUSE	(52) Phoenix LP12

CHARLIE PARKER WITH STRINGS

Chris Griffin, Al Porcino, Bernie Privin (tp), Will Bradley, Bill Harris (tb), Charlie Parker, Toots Mondello, Murray Williams (as), Hank Ross, Art Drellinger (ts), Stan Webb (bs), unknown strings, Verley Mills (harp), Lou Stein (p), Art Ryerson (g), Bob Haggart (b), Don Lamond (d), Joe Lippman (arr, cond). *NYC, January 23, 1952*

675-2	TEMPTATION	(53) Mercury/Clef 11088
676-3	LOVER	(53) Mercury/Clef 11089
677-4	AUTUMN IN NEW.YORK	(53) Mercury/Clef 11088
678-4	STELLA BY STARLIGHT	(53) Mercury/Clef 11089

CHARLIE PARKER QUINTET

Benny Harris (tp), Charlie Parker (as), Walter Bishop (p), Teddy Kotick (b), Max Roach (d), Luis Miranda (cga). *NYC, January 28, 1952*

679-4	MAMA INEZ	(53) Mercury/Clef 11092
680-3	LA CUCARACHA	(53) Mercury/Clef 11093
681-5	ESTRELLITA	(53) Mercury/Clef 11094
682-3	BEGIN THE BEGUINE -1	(53) Mercury/Clef 11094
683-1	LA PALOMA	(53) Mercury/Clef 11091

1- Harris out

CHARLIE PARKER BIG BAND

Jimmy Maxwell, Carl Poole, Al Porcino, Bernie Privin (tp), Bill Harris, Lou McGarity, Bart Varsalona (tb), Charlie Parker, Harry Terrill, Murray Williams (as), Flip Phillips, Hank Ross (ts), Danny Bank (bs), Oscar Peterson (p), Freddie Green (g), Ray Brown (b), Don Lamond (d), Joe Lippman (arr, cond). *NYC, March 25, 1952*

756-5	NIGHT AND DAY	(53) Mercury/Clef 11096
757-4	ALMOST LIKE BEING IN LOVE	(53) Mercury/Clef 11102
758-1	I CAN'T GET STARTED	(53) Mercury/Clef 11096
759-5	WHAT IS THIS THING CALLED LOVE	(53) Mercury/Clef 11102

CHARLIE PARKER

Dizzy Gillespie (tp), Charlie Parker (as), Billy Taylor (p), Charles Mingus (b), Max Roach (d). *NYC, c. spring 1952*

	HOW HIGH THE MOON	Klacto MG102

	HOT HOUSE	Klacto MG102
	EMBRACEABLE YOU	Klacto MG102

JAM SESSION

Charlie Shavers (tp), Benny Carter, Johnny Hodges, Charlie Parker (as), Flip Phillips, Ben Webster (ts), Oscar Peterson (p), Barney Kessel (g), Ray Brown (b), J. C. Heard (d). *LA, June 1952.*

802-2	JAM BLUES	(54) Clef MGC601
803-3	WHAT IT THIS THING CALLED LOVE	(54) Clef MGC602
804-2	BALLAD MEDLEY	(54) Clef MGC601
805-2	FUNKY BLUES	(54) Clef MGC602

Note: Parker's solo feature on BALLAD MEDLEY is DEARLY BELOVED.

CHARLIE PARKER

Chet Baker (tp), Charlie Parker, Sonny Criss (as), Al Haig -1, Russ Freeman -2 (p), Harry Babasin (b), Lawrence Marable (d). *Trade Winds Club, LA, June 16, 1952*

THE SQUIRREL -1	(55) Jazz Showcase 5007
UNKOWN TITLE	(55) Jazz Showcase 5007
THEY DIDN'T BELIEVE ME -1	
INDIANA -2	(55) Jazz Showcase 5007
LIZA -1	(55) Jazz Showcase 5007

Charlie Parker (p), Duke Jordan (p), Charles Mingus (b), Phil Brown (d). *Birdland, NYC, September 20, 1952.*

ORNITHOLOGY	Mark MG101
52ND STREET THEME	Mark MG101

Charlie Parker (as), unknown ob and strings -1, Walter Bishop (p), Mundell Lowe (g), Teddy Kotick (b), Max Roach (d). *Rockland Palace NYC, September 26, 1952.*

ROCKER -1	(29,56) Charlie Parker PLP401
MOOSE THE MOOCHE	(29,56) Charlie Parker PLP401
JUST FRIENDS	(56) Charlie Parker CP(2)502
MY LITTLE SUEDE SHOES	(56) Charlie Parker PLP401
I'LL REMEMBER APRIL -1	(56) Charlie Parker CP(2)502
SLY MONGOOSE	(56) Charlie Parker PLP401
LAURA -1	(56) Charlie Parker PLP401
STAR EYES	(56) Charlie Parker PLP401
THIS TIME THE DREAM'S ON ME	(56) Charlie Parker PLP401
EASY TO LOVE -1	(56) Charlie Parker CP(2)502
COOL BLUES	(29,56) Charlie Parker PLP401
WHAT IS THIS THING CALLED LOVE	(56) Charlie Parker CP(2)502

I DIDN'T KNOW WHAT TIME IT WAS	(56) Charlie Parker CP(2)502	
REPETITION -1	(56) Charlie Parker CP(2)502	
LESTER LEAPS IN	(56) Charlie Parker PLP401	
EAST OF THE SUN -1	(56) Charlie Parker CP(2)502	
APRIL IN PARIS -1	(56) Charlie Parker CP(2)502	
OUT OF NOWHERE -1	(56) Charlie Parker CP(2)502	
ROCKER -1	(56) Charlie Parker CP(2)502	

Charlie Parker (as), John Lewis (p), Milt Jackson (vib), Percy Heath (b), Kenny Clarke (d). *Birdland, NYC, November 1, 1952*

HOW HIGH THE MOON	Mark MG101
EMBRACEABLE YOU	Mark MG101
52ND STREET (theme)	Mark MG101

Charlie Parker (as), unknown ob and strings, Walter Bishop (p), Walter Yost (b), Roy Haynes (d), Candido (cga-1). *Carnegie Hall, NYC, November 14, 1952.*

JUST FRIENDS	FDC1005
EASY TO LOVE	(45) FDC1005
REPETITION -1	(45) FDC1006
NIGHT IN TUNISIA -1,2	(45) FDC1006
52ND STREET THEME -1,2	(45) FDC1006

2- Dizzy Gillespie (tp) replaces ob and strings.

CHARLIE PARKER QUARTET

Charlie Parker (as), Hank Jones (p), Teddy Kotick (b), Max Roach (d). *NYC, December 30, 1952*

1118-3	THE SONG IS YOU (I HEAR MUSIC)	(53) Clef 89144
1119-7	LAIRD BAIRD	(53) Clef 89144
1120-2	KIM	(53) Verve MGV8005
1120-4	KIM	Clef 89129
1121-2	COSMIC RAYS	(53) Clef 89129
1121-5	COSMIC RAYS	Verve MGV8005

MILES DAVIS

Miles Davis (tp), Sonny Rollins, Charlie Parker (ts), Walter Bishop (p), Percy Heath (b), Philly Joe Jones (d). *NYC, January 30, 1953*

450	COMPULSION	(57) Prestige PRLP7044
451-1	SERPENT'S TOOTH	(57) Prestige PRLP7044
451-2	SERPENT'S TOOTH	(57) Prestige PRLP7044
452	'ROUND MIDNIGHT	(57) Prestige PRLP7044

CHARLIE PARKER

Bill Harris (tb), Charlie Mariano, Charlie Parker (as), Harry Johnson (ts), Sonny Truitt (p), Chubby Jackson (b), Morey Feld (d), band vcl. *Birdland, NYC, February 16, 1953*

YOUR FATHER'S MOUSTACHE v	(34) Queen-Disc Q-002

Charlie Parker (as) with 'The Orchestra': Ed Leddy, Marky Markowitz, Charlie Walp, Bob Carey (tp), Earl Swope, Rob Swope, Don Spiker (tbn), Jim Riley (as),

Angelo Tompros, Jim Parker, Ben Lary (ts), Jack Nimitz (bs), Jack Holliday (p,arr) Mert Oliver (d), Joe Timer (d,arr), Bill Potts, Gerry Mulligan, Al Cohn, Johnny Mandel (arr). *Club Kavakos, Washington, February 22, 1953*

FINE AND DANDY	(58) Musician E1–60019
THESE FOOLISH THINGS	(58) Musician E1–60019
LIGHT GREEN	(58) Musician E1–60019
THOU SWELL	(58) Musician E1–60019
WILLIS	(58) Musician E1–60019
DON'T BLAME ME	(58) Musician E1–60019**
SOMETHING TO REMEMBER YOU BY/BLUE ROOM	(58) Musician E1–60019
ROUNDHOUSE	(58) Musician E1–60019

Charlie Parker (as), unknown p,g,b,d. *Howard Theatre, Washington, same period.*

COOL BLUES	(59) VGM VGM0009
OUT OF NOWHERE	(59) VGM VGM0009
ORNITHOLOGY	(59) VGM VGM0009
ANTHROPOLOGY	(59) VGM VGM0009
SCRAPPLE FROM THE APPLE	(59) VGM VGM0009
OUT OF NOWHERE	(59) VGM VGM0009
NOW'S THE TIME -1	(59) VGM VGM0009

1- unknown tp, tb, ts added.

Charlie Parker (as), Brew Moore (ts), Paul Bley (p), Dick Garcia (g), Neil Michel (b), Ted Pastor (d). *Montreal, c. March 1953*

COOL BLUES	Jazz Showcase 5003
BERNIE'S TUNE	Jazz Showcase 5003
DON'T BLAME ME	Jazz Showcase 5003
WAHOO	Jazz Showcase 5003

Valdo Williams (p), Hal Gaylor (b), Billy Graham (d) replace Moore, Bley, Michel and Pastor. *Same location and date.*

ORNITHOLOGY	Jazz Showcase 5003
EMBRACEABLE YOU	Jazz Showcase 5003

Charlie Parker (as), Milt Buckner (org), Bernie McKay (g), Cornelius Thomas (d). *Birdland, NYC, March 23, 1953*

GROOVIN' HIGH	(34,49) Queen-Disc Q-002

Charlie Parker (as), Walter Bishop (p), Kenny O'Brien (b), Roy Haynes (d). *Bandbox, NYC, March 30, 1953*

CARAVAN (theme)	Klacto MG100
STAR EYES	(34) Klacto MG100
ORNITHOLOGY	(34) Klacto MG100
DIGGIN' DIZ	(34) Klacto MG100
EMBRACEABLE YOU	(34) Klacto MG100

Charlie Parker (as), John Lewis (p), Curley Russell (b), Kenny Clarke (d), Candido (cga -1). *Birdland, NYC, May 9, 1953*

COOL BLUES	(49) Klacto MG100
STAR EYES	(49) Klacto MG100
MOOSE THE MOOCHE	(49) Klacto MG100
LULLABY OF BIRDLAND (theme)	(49) Klacto MG100
BROADWAY -1	(49) Klacto MG100
LULLABY OF BIRDLAND (theme) -1	(49) Klacto MG100

THE QUINTET OF THE YEAR
Dizzy Gillespie (tp,vcl), Charlie Parker (as), Bud Powell (p), Charles Mingus (b), Max Roach (d). *Massey Hall, Toronto, May 15, 1953*

	WEE (i.e. ALLEN'S ALLEY)	(60) Debut DLP4
	HOT HOUSE	(60) Debut DLP4
	NIGHT IN TUNISIA	(60) Debut DLP4
	PERDIDO	(60) Debut DLP2
	SALT PEANUTS vDG	(60) Debut DLP2
	ALL THE THE THINGS YOU ARE/52ND STREET THEME	(60) Debut DLP2

CHARLIE PARKER AND HIS ORCHESTRA
Junior Collins (fr-h), Charlie Parker (as), Al Block (f), Hal McKusick (cl), Tommy Mace (ob), Manny Thaler (bsn), Tony Aless (p), Charles Mingus (b), Max Roach (d), Dave Lambert Singers (vcl), Gil Evans (arr,cond). *NYC, May 22, 1953*

1238-7	IN THE STILL OF THE NIGHT	(53) Clef 11100
1239-9	OLD FOLKS	(53) Clef 11100
1240-9	IF I LOVE AGAIN	(53) Verve MGV8009

BUD POWELL TRIO WITH CHARLIE PARKER
Charlie Parker (as), Bud Powell (p), Charles Mingus (b), Art Taylor (d), Candido (cga-1) *Birdland, NYC, May 30, 1953.*

	MOOSE THE MOOCHE -1	(34,61) Queen-Disc Q-002
	CHERYL -1	(34,61) Queen-Disc Q-002

Max Roach (d) replaces Taylor. *Same period.*

	DANCE OF THE INFIDELS	(34) Parktec 4627-1

DIZZY GILLESPIE QUINTET WITH CHARLIE PARKER
Dizzy Gillespie, Miles Davis -1 (tp), Charlie Parker (as), Sahib Shihab (bs), Wade Legge (p), Lou Hackney (b), Al Jones (d), Joe Carroll (vcl). *Birdland, NYC, c. June 1953.*

	THE BLUEST BLUES vJC -1	Klacto MG102
	ON THE SUNNY SIDE OF THE STREET vJC	Klacto MG102

CHARLIE PARKER QUARTET
Charlie Parker (as), Al Haig (p), Percy Heath (b), Max Roach (d). *NYC, August 4, 1953*

1246-1	CHI CHI	Verve MGV8005
1246-3	CHI CHI	(53) Verve MGV8005
1246-6	CHI CHI	Clef 89138
1247-3	I REMEMBER YOU	(53) Clef 89138
1248-1	NOW'S THE TIME	(53)Clef MGC517
1249-3	CONFIRMATION	(53) Clef MGC517

CHARLIE PARKER
Herbie Williams (tp), Charlie Parker (as), Rollins Griffith (p), Jimmy Woode (b), Marquis Foster (d). *Hi Hat, Boston, December 19/20, 1953.*

	NOW'S THE TIME	(62) Phoenix LP10

ORNITHOLOGY	(62) Phoenix LP10
MY LITTLE SUEDE SHOES	(62) Phoenix LP10
GROOVIN' HIGH	(62) Phoenix LP10
CHERYL	(62) Phoenix LP10*
ORNITHOLOGY	(62) Phoenix LP10*

Hi Hat, Boston, January 24, 1954.

COOL BLUES	(52) Phoenix LP12
MY LITTLE SUEDE SHOES	(52) Phoenix LP12*
ORNITHOLOGY	(52) Phoenix LP12
OUT OF NOWHERE	(52) Phoenix LP12
JUMPIN' WITH SYMPHONY SID	(52) Phoenix LP12

CHARLIE PARKER WITH STAN KENTON
Charlie Parker (as) with Sam Noto, Vic Minichelli, Buddy Childers, Stu Williamson, Don Smith (tp), Milt Gold, Joe Ciavardone, Frank Rosolino, George Roberts (tb), Charlie Mariano, Dave Schildkraut, (as), Mike Cicchetti, Bill Perkins (ts), Tony Ferina (bs), Stan Kenton (p), Bob Lesher (g), Don Bagley (b), Stan Levey (d), Bill Holman (arr).*Civic Auditorium, Portland, February 25, 1954*

NIGHT AND DAY	(63) Jazz Supreme JS703
MY FUNNY VALENTINE	(63) Jazz Supreme JS703
CHEROKEE	(63) Jazz Supreme JS703

CHARLIE PARKER QUINTET
Charlie Parker (as), Walter Bishop (p), Jerome Darr (g), Teddy Kotick (b), Roy Haynes (d). *NYC, March 31, 1954*

1531-2	I GET A KICK OUT OF YOU	Verve MGV8007
1531-7	I GET A KICK OUT OF YOU -1	(53) Verve MGV8007
1532-1	JUST ONE OF THOSE THINGS -1	(53) Verve MGV 8007
1533-2	MY HEART BELONGS TO DADDY -1	(53) Verve MGV8007
1534-1	I'VE GOT YOU UNDER MY SKIN	(53) Verve MGV8007

CHARLIE PARKER
Charlie Parker (as), unknown strings, prob. Walter Bishop (p), unknown b,d. *Birdland, NYC, August 27, 1954*

WHAT IS THIS THING CALLED LOVE	Spook Jazz SPJ6604
REPETITION	Spook Jazz SPJ6604
EASY TO LOVE	Spook Jazz SPJ6604
EAST OF THE SUN	Spook Jazz SPJ6604

Charlie Parker (as), John Lewis (p), Percy Heath (b), Kenny Clarke (d). *Carnegie Hall, NYC, September 25, 1954*

THE SONG IS YOU	(64) Roulette RE127
MY FUNNY VALENTINE	(64) Roulette RE127
COOL BLUES	(64) Roulette RE127

CHARLIE PARKER QUINTET
Charlie Parker (as), Walter Bishop (p), Billy Bauer (g), Teddy Kotick (b), Art Taylor (d). *NYC, December 10, 1954.*

2115-4	LOVE FOR SALE	Verve MGV8007
2115-5	LOVE FOR SALE	(53) Verve MGV8001
2116-2	I LOVE PARIS	Verve MGV8007
2116-3	I LOVE PARIS	(53) Verve MGV8001

INDEX TO DISCOGRAPHY

Recently available albums are shown here with American catalogue numbers first (if any) and, where different, European issues afterwards; basic recommended albums are those **printed in bold type**. Since continued availability is always a problem, it is advisable to use a knowledgeable jazz record shop such as those that advertise in jazz periodicals, and they may often be able to locate items only obtainable second-hand.

Bibliography

Feather, Leonard: *From Satchmo to Miles*. New York, Stein and Day; London, Quartet.

Gitler, Ira: *Jazz Masters of the 40's*. New York, Macmillan; London, Collier.

Harrison, Max: *Charlie Parker*. London, Cassell; New York, A. S. Barnes.

Hentoff, Nat: *Jazz Is*. New York, Random House; London, W. H. Allen.

Parker, Chan, and Paudras, Francis: *To Bird with Love*. Poitiers, Editions Wizlov.

Reisner, Robert: *Bird: the Legend of Charlie Parker*. New York, Da Capo; London, Quartet.

Russell, Ross: *Bird Lives!* New York, Charter House; London, Quartet.

Watts, Charlie: *Ode to a Highflying Bird*. London, Beat Publications.

Williams, Martin: *The Jazz Tradition*. New York and London, Oxford U.P.

The first book to be published on Parker was Max Harrison's short critical study in 1960 which, although superseded in some factual details, concentrates on the music and as such stands up extremely well. Reisner, after several years of research, chose to print in 1962 a series of statements by over 80 interviewees, giving a kaleidoscopic and appropriately complex view of his subject. Ten years later, Ross Russell drew heavily on this source but filled out a convincing portrait of the man and his times which, despite annoying minor errors of a musical or chronological nature, is likely to remain the definitive full-length biography. The expensive coffee-table book by Chan Parker and designer Francis Paudras, though containing nuggets of information, is something of a curio for collectors (as, in a rather different way, was the tiny volume by Rolling Stones drummer Watts).

The relevant chapters in the books by Gitler, Hentoff, Williams and Feather place Parker in the context of the jazz scene as a whole. Along with the first three items discussed, they not only provided most of the material in this book but are the most valuable choices for further reading.